Reunions
for
Fun-Loving
Families

MINA-LUNING BRANCH LIBRARY
P.O. BOX 143
MINA, NV 89422

OKS ... *for living life well!*

Nancy Funke Bagley

PRINTED IN UNITED STATES OF AMERICA

BRIGHTON PUBLICATIONS

Brighton Publications, Inc.
P.O. Box 120706
St. Paul, MN 55112-0706
612-636-2220

First Edition: 1994

Library of Congress Cataloging-in-Publication Data
Bagley, Nancy Funke
    Reunions for fun-loving families / Nancy Funke Bagley. — 1st ed.
        p.   cm.
    Includes index.
    1. Family reunions—United States—Planning.   I. Title.
GT2423.B34   1994   94-11405
394.2–dc20   CIP
                        ISBN 0-918420-21-0

Printed in the United States of America

To my husband, Richard
and
my parents, Don and Norma

TABLE OF CONTENTS

Day Fun / Evening Fun / Mealtime / Professional Planners / A Cruise / Hotel, Motel, or Resort / Family Entertainment / The Talent List

10 GUEST OF HONOR / 71

Single out one person or a group for special fanfare during the day. This can be the start of a family tradition family that will highlight every reunion.

Choosing the Guest of Honor / Notifying the Guest of Honor / Reminiscing Time / Thoughtful Tributes / For Those Not Present / Celebrating Babies / Introducing Spouses / Honor the Reunion Planners

11 THEMES / 76

Now it's time for the fun stuff. Picking a theme for your reunion is just what your party needs. These detailed themes are planned around easily accessible reunion sites.

Western Barbecue / Luau / Sock Hop / Black and White Semi-Formal / Zoo Safari / Family Heritage Feast / Carnival Time

12 THEME STARTERS / 88

Here are more helpful ideas to get you started on the path of creative inspiration. Modify them as you will to fit your family reunion.

Travel Treasures / Super Bowl Winner / Chili Cook-Off / House Project / Celebrate the Oldest and the Youngest / Relay-Race Runs / Hollywood Stars / Vintage Year / Time Capsule / Old Tyme Kitchen Party

13 LET'S DO IT AGAIN / 95

Reunions are habit forming. To make the next reunion a success, you'll need to do some planning now.

Picking the Date / The Next Reunion Site / Suggestions for Improvement / New Planning Ideas / The Next Chairperson / Transfer the Information / Announce All Decisions / Lack of Interest / Family Newsletter / Mini-Reunion

14 UPDATE THE FAMILY STORY / 101

A family reunion gives everyone the opportunity to catch up on family news. An easy way to make sure everyone hears the news is to have each family member answer a planned list of questions. Collect the questionnaires and make a booklet. Give the booklet to the members of the family.

Questionnaires / Ask Appropriate Questions / Make the Questions Fun / Questionnaire Samples / Best Time / Who Can't Attend / Presenting the Information / Extra Copies / When to Give Out the Booklets / The Questionnaire As a Reunion Activity

Every reunion has its own perplexing moments. You'll find the answers here may encourage you to tackle your unique questions.

Pets / Professional Photographer / Inexpensive Photographs / Family Chefs / Religious Family Members / Computer Help / Loaning Car to Relatives / Entertaining Relatives / Teenagers / A Necessary Reunion Ingredient

A Family Tree Diagram / Expense Logs / Invitation Examples / Invitation Log

REAL PEOPLE, REAL REUNIONS

Keeping in contact with my immediate family is important to me. But there are also times I want to meet distant relatives or find out more about my family tree. Attending a family reunion provides the perfect occasion to get to know both close and distant relatives better.

I find planning the family reunion to be a wonderful experience. Like planning any big party, it takes effort. But, the rewards are tremendous. It's a pleasure to see generations coming together to meet each other, share family memories and just have fun.

There are as many kinds of reunions as there are families. The reunion can be planned for months or be a spur-of-the-moment affair. The important thing is getting the family together.

While writing this book, I came across many people willing to discuss their reunions. I have chosen five of these stories to illustrate various reunion styles. All of these reunions were wonderful, exciting events for both the planners and the participants.

PLANNING A REUNION IS CHILD'S PLAY

Proving that where there's a will there's a way, Nancy Grimm of Cut Bank, Montana planned a reunion for eighty people when she was fifteen years old. "My grandma, Eva Fugle, was ill and it had been ten years since both sides of the family were together. There had been talk of a get-together for years. so I decided to be the one to organize the reunion. My mom helped me gather names and addresses of relatives she knew and those she didn't know we got from grandma."

Nancy held her reunion in the city park (which had a first come—first to use policy) so it would be easily found by relatives. Once she knew where the reunion would be held, Nancy designed construction paper invitations issued in her name. "It was kind of funny because the relatives were calling in their responses but they didn't have a clue as to who sent the invitation. Although married, my mom was still thought of as Betty Fugle in the family, so the relatives had no idea who Nancy Grimm was."

Nancy, though only fifteen, had an after-school job and was able to pay for all the pre-reunion expenses. "I just knew if I didn't organize the reunion, it wouldn't get done. I really wanted to see the families together so I did what was necessary to make it happen.'

On the invitation, Nancy asked her relatives to bring specific food to pass. As a fifteen year old, she asked them to bring *her* favorites. For those that were traveling from out of town, Nancy requested paper plates, disposable silverware, and watermelon. Everyone was more than willing to cooperate.

Reunion day arrived, and so did the relatives. The main activity of the day was a baseball game. Nancy remembers playing that game for hours and hours. Every adult and child was involved and the game seemed to go on forever.

After the meal, the adults sat around and visited with each other while the children amused themselves with water activities. "These activities involved us kids hiding behind bushes and throwing balloons and cups of water on each other and eventually the grown-ups. I remember the water was taken away when an aunt got her hair soaked and my mom decided we'd had enough fun for one day!"

Nancy's reunion proves that family members will get together and enjoy each other if someone will just organize the party. A fifteen year old, with limited funds, was able to orchestrate a reunion for a family that hadn't gotten together in ten years and hasn't gotten together since.

AN EVERY YEAR AFFAIR

Rick Torres of Anaheim, California was instrumental in planning the most recent "Rivera" family reunion in Southern California. The Rivera family, consisting of 500 plus members, has yearly reunions scheduled for Saturday and Sunday of Labor Day weekend. Four years in a row the reunions are held in Salt Lake City, Utah. On the fifth year, the reunion is moved to California. "When the reunion is held in California, my relatives incorporate the reunion with their vacation. We include hotel and motel lists (with prices), as well as brochures of tourist attractions with the invitations. We also note who has room in their homes to take in out-of-town relatives."

Reunion information was sent out at three different times. Four months prior to the reunion, family members received a flyer announcing the upcoming reunion and asking for names and addresses of missing relatives. At two months, a letter was sent announcing the location of the reunion weekend activities. A month before, relatives were asked to call in and confirm their attendance. At this time a schedule of events was sent so everyone knew exactly what activities were planned.

When questioned regarding the financing of such a large undertaking, Torres explained the necessity of a reunion committee to share the costs. "We view this as a family activity with everyone contributing in a way that is best for them, as well as the family. If you're able to handle the printing, you volunteer for that project. If you're better able to handle the postage costs, you offer your services in that area. We also realize some people are better able to contribute time rather than money, so they are given responsibilities involving setting up or cleaning up. We don't experience problems because we all *want* to be involved in this reunion since it keeps our family together."

Day one of the reunion was picnic day for the Rivera family. "Children outnumber adults three to one, so this is their day. Games are planned for four to six hours followed by the pot luck meal. Since we're of Mexican heritage, the big activity of the day is having the children break the piñata (a paper maché cartoon character filled with candy and trinkets)." Torres pointed out that while the games took place, the planning committee was walking around introducing themselves and family members to each other. With a crowd the size of theirs, you'll often have relatives who haven't met each other.

The second day of the reunion began with a church service for those who cared to attend, and was followed by a brunch. The reunion committee financed the meal, and it was prepared by an uncle. "I was stationed at the bottom of the driveway and checked off the names of people as they arrived for the meal. We used this as an opportunity to update our mailing list as well as keeping track of attendance. The Riveras used the time after the meal for family activities. These included giving small gifts to the oldest and youngest members attending and those with the most children. The next order of business was the traditional telling of how the family came up from Mexico and settled in Utah and California. A chart with the original sisters and brothers is displayed as a visual aid during this recitation.

Torres had some interesting comments to share regarding reunion souvenirs and family traditions. "We initially gave away T-shirts as our souvenirs and discovered that with our large crowd, and not knowing everyone's size, T-shirts just didn't work. When we changed our gift to hats, where one size fits all, we had a happier crowd. Second, in regard to family traditions, don't try something new without careful thought. One year the planners chose to feed everyone a fast food fried chicken instead of a traditional Mexican meal. It just didn't feel right and there were a lot of disappointed family members."

SHARING THE WORK

After a conversation with Mim Gibson of Cerritos, California, I wanted to run right out and plan a reunion. Mim has a delightful way of describing the three day "Karstad" reunions, which are successful because of cooperation within her family.

The Karstad reunions had been taking place every four years, but because of their success, will soon be changed to three year intervals. The reunions rotate between California and Minnesota so when the reunion takes place in your state, all visitors are considered guests. The reunion responsibilities are handled and organized only by local family members.

"We are fortunate that our family is large enough to divide the tasks according to major activities. This year I was in charge of planning, purchasing for, and preparing the Saturday brunch. I decorated the table in the colors of the Norwegian flag, coordinating the tablecloth, napkins, and fresh flowers. I enjoyed every minute of my area of responsibility and took great pride in making sure every detail was perfect. Every bit of time and expense was worthwhile in presenting a lovely brunch to my family."

The novel aspect of the Karstad reunion is that because you have total responsibility for only one event, you are able to enjoy the rest of the weekend. Other events at the most recent reunion included a Friday beach party, barbecue and street dance, a Saturday night formal dinner, and a Sunday baseball game. Because each activity was assigned to one person, it was a matter of pride to make it successful.

The yearly speeches and tributes took place at the formal dinner on Saturday. In addition to family members, special non-related friends were included in this activity. Everyone was encouraged to speak and afterward the master of ceremonies passed out slips of paper which contained the name of a brother or sister. Each person choosing a name had to get up in turn and tell a story involving the person who's name they picked.

"We also began a new family tradition this year involving the 'Karstad Ruby' which was part of a necklace acquired by a cousin during the previous reunion. He took it apart and mounted the stone on velvet and presented it to the 'relative doing the most for the family reunion'. This person must now prominently display it in their home until the next reunion when they'll pass it on. This will become a meaningful tradition because it promotes family participation."

Mim's family also has a unique way of housing the out-of-town relatives. Each local person takes in a family for the week and is responsible for their meals and entertainment. This is agreeable to all concerned because the same will be done for them when they travel to the next reunion. All family members are close enough to want to share their homes with each other.

The biggest concern when this family gets together is finding enough time to do all the planned activities. Because of this, for the next reunion, they're going to look into a campground or resort where meals are provided. "We've discovered we spend a large portion of our time cooking and cleaning up our meals. We're at a point in our reunions where we're willing to have someone else handle those chores so we can have more time to get to know each other better. We find there are many things we want to do and not nearly enough time."

Mim and her family are proof that if everyone does just one portion of the planning, a wonderful event will grow. The fact that everyone looks forward to the reunion and takes pride in the family insures many years of happy get-togethers.

EXTENDING THE REUNION

Sally Somsel of Traverse City, Michigan described a very creative idea that came out of the last "Milliron" family reunion. While attending the annual picnic in the town where the family originally settled, it was discovered that the next town over, Thompsonville, was going to be having a centennial celebration in two weeks. Sally and her family decided to participate in that event by building a float symbolizing the family history.

"We had two weeks to design and build a float so we organized a group of thirty-five relatives and made this our chief goal. We spent many hours building a replica of the towns' one room schoolhouse. More importantly, we spent those same hours telling family stories and enjoying each others company."

On parade day, family members met to ride on the float and march in the parade. Colored ribbons were issued indicating which family branch the relatives belonged to. Some family members had one ribbon and others had three, depending on how many ways they were related.

The parade was a success and so was the Milliron clan. "It was quite exciting to be named the top float in the parade. We especially considered this an honor because it was an extension of our family and family reunion." The rest of the day was spent participating in the centennial activities and enjoying the family once again.

This activity is a good example of extending an ordinary pot-luck reunion into a moment of family pride by being willing to give a little extra effort. Their first place honors in the parade will be the subject of photos and talk for many reunions to come.

OVERNIGHT CAMPING IS FUN FOR KIDS

My family would never forgive me if I didn't talk about our yearly reunion. For the past eight years the "Funke" family has gotten together for the annual summer camp-out. A site within an hour of where the family lives is chosen and the fun begins after work on Friday.

On Friday there is a quick dinner and the setting up of camp. No children are permitted at this time unless they are accompanied by their own parent. This has been considered primarily an adult only night.

Saturday morning begins with a large breakfast—cooked by the men in the family. About eleven o'clock, family members who were unable to stay the night arrive. The dinner turkey is set up on the barbecue, books and lounge chairs are opened, and water balloons fly. In the afternoon, miniature golf competitions take place. After the evening meal, at about 6:30 P.M., those not spending the night leave.

Parents are encouraged to allow their children over the age of five to spend the night, even if they go home. The evening activities include pinball at the clubhouse and sitting around a campfire telling family stories. The children use this opportunity to ask questions and learn more about their parents when they were young. The evening ends with a marshmallow roast over the barely lit fire embers. Everyone goes to bed at the same time because there is no way the kids are going to sleep if there is any activity by the adults. This is their big night out and they don't intend to waste any time sleeping if they can help it! Though never needed, all parents who leave children are *required* to also leave an insurance card and a note giving emergency room personnel permission to treat their child in case of an accident.

Everyone, including the children, are asked to bring something. A young child may be asked to bring a toothbrush (their own) or a sleeping bag (their own) because we believe it teaches them to be responsible. When they see their name on the list, along with the adults, the children feel they are a necessary part of the reunion activities.

Sunday is spent having a nice breakfast and cleaning up the camp. Everyone is required to help, regardless of age. After that, it's time to gather the kids and head home.

2

You Have to
Start Somewhere!

*Y*ou've decided that a family reunion is a good idea, but as with any good idea, someone has to make it work. You'll either want to take on the role yourself or ask family members to be part of a committee to divide up all the tasks that need to be done. Or, you may decide to make the decisions yourself but delegate the specific jobs that need to be completed. Any of these options will work. This chapter will discuss the good and bad points of an individual planner, planning by committee, and having a reunion coordinator.

One Planner

The best thing about a one person planning committee is that decisions can be made and implemented immediately. In the process of planning a reunion, decisions are often based on the domino effect. The location can't be determined until the size of the crowd is estimated and the size of the crowd can't be estimated until you figure out how many generations you're going to invite. A lone planner can sit down, make these decisions in a minute or two, and get to the next topic.

Most people who are confident enough to plan a reunion are aware of the immediate decisions that need to be made. If you're the only planner, you can make quick decisions and not spend time discussing topics you consider irrelevant. Some people have a habit of getting so involved in discussing details they never get around to the larger picture. If you're the only planner, you save yourself the aggravation of trying to find a consensus or compromise. It's not uncommon for a committee to get stuck on a minor issue and spend a whole meeting getting back on track. Remember, an elephant is often described as a horse designed by a committee.

No Scheduling Conflicts

If you're a committee of one, you only have to worry about your schedule and not the schedules of others. Depending on the committee size and its current priorities, you can lose valuable time trying to find an opportunity to get together. This will prolong the planning phase, especially if each committee member insists on being involved in every decision.

As the sole planner of the family reunion, no one else knows what you've scheduled. Suppose in your timetable of events, a baseball game was scheduled for 11:00 A.M. Unexpectedly, at 10:45 P.M. twenty of the guests decide they want to organize a basketball tournament. Since only you know baseball is to begin in fifteen minutes, and basketball was scheduled for later, you can accommodate the guests. If more people knew of the agenda, you might feel obligated to stick to the schedule as planned, rather than allowing the guests to be spontaneous. Also, as the sole planner, there is no such thing as a mistake; if anyone asks, everything is going just as you anticipated.

The sole planner will have to deal with those who feel they could have done better. As long as you feel you are doing everything properly, you can maintain a positive attitude and ignore them. Respond to their comments in the following manner:

"I appreciate your interest, but everything is under control"

"It seems to be working this way, so why change something that isn't broken."

"Write down all the changes you feel should be made. When it's your turn to be in charge you'll know exactly what to do."

DRAWBACKS OF THE SOLE PLANNER

The major disadvantage of planning the reunion alone is you are in fact alone! You are completely on your own to do everything from conceiving the idea to planning, inviting, financing, and entertaining. While your ideas may be excellent, input from others may suggest options that hadn't occurred to you. Additionally, involving other family members spreads out the work load as well as the financial responsibility.

PLANNING BY COMMITTEE

The more people involved in a project, the more ideas the group will develop. Sometimes you need a variety of perspectives when tackling a big project such as planning a family reunion. During initial brainstorming sessions, you'll be grateful for the different points of view—and wonder if you'd have ever thought of some of the brilliant options.

The planning process will be enhanced if you have both men and women on the planning committee. Men may be wary of such an assignment, but their input will be valuable. They'll be able to offer suggestions on how to get men to the party and how to entertain them once they arrive. Take advantage of the diversity in your family.

The reunion will also benefit if you include participants in the planning process with whom you have only a passing acquaintance. Ask relatives you rarely communicate with or hardly know at all to become part of the planning committee. This not only acquaints you with someone new, but will give insight as to what other branches of the family expect from such a gathering. One is better able to handle different entertainment expectations if they are discovered in the initial planning stages. If the King branch enjoys large spreads of home cooking, and the Williams branch would prefer take-out hamburgers, the group needs to come to a compromise before going further into the reunion planning. Family idiosyncrasies, large or small, need to be identified, accepted, and accommodated.

No one knows better than a fifty-five year old how a middle aged person wants to be entertained. By the same token, someone fifty-five isn't necessarily the best person to prepare the agenda for teenagers. Children are great to have on the committee because they enjoy the attention and don't mind doing the licking, folding, and other disagreeable tasks. It's important to include every age group on the committee to best understand the tastes of that generation.

Share Responsibilities

The committee has the job of handling the reunion from start to finish. The time span from conceiving the idea of having a reunion to resting up the day afterward may be many months. During those months, there are numerous arrangements to be made, plans to follow up, expenses to be met, and frustrations to be expected. As part of a committee, all of this can be shared.

Committee Size

The size of the committee will be influenced by the type of reunion being planned and how many people are necessary to achieve the desired results. If the committee is too large, nothing will be accomplished due to prolonged discussion of the issues. If the committee is too small, those participating may become overwhelmed by the work to be done.

Member Commitment

Don't allow a few people to carry the bulk of the work because some committee members are unable or unwilling to fully participate. You must be sure each prospective committee member understands their commitment to the group. It's best to realistically describe all the tasks to be done so potential committee members won't later feel they were misled doing something they didn't fully grasp.

Overzealous Members

A committee functions best when all its members feel welcome to contribute and communicate their ideas. The strongest, most articulate, and opinionated members of the group will often take over. Initially it may seem easier to allow these people to dominate, but over time the committee will cease to function as a group.

A good way of dealing with an opinionated committee member is to designate them note taker at the meetings. As the chairperson calls on the committee members, the note taker is responsible for writing down their contribution. It's very hard to dominate a discussion while also taking meaningful notes!

A TEASPOON OF SUGAR

As the chairperson of the reunion committee, you can put some fun into the planning process. Purchase brightly colored folders for everyone to keep track of the reunion paperwork; plan committee meetings at interesting restaurants (possibly a different nationality for each meeting); and give everyone a T-shirt to wear to the meetings that states "happiness…is planning the South family reunion".

On reunion day, present a small gift to your committee members for all of their help and dedication. This could be an engraved cup with the reunion date, a gift certificate to their favorite restaurant or a neatly penned letter of appreciation. A little bit of creativity and fun will turn the work into fond memories for the committee participants.

THE COORDINATOR

This is an ideal solution for the take-charge person who doesn't want to do everything alone. This person will make the basic decisions such as time, location, and theme and then appoint members of the family to work out the details. For example, once a park theme is chosen by the coordinator, another person is assigned the task of finding the most convenient park and confirming its availability. It's important the assistants understand that when differences in opinion can't be resolved, the coordinator will make the final decision.

Committee Tasks

Whether there is one reunion planner or a committee, certain decisions need to be made. The sooner these topics are addressed and a time frame for completing each project is estimated, the sooner the reunion date can be set. All of these topics will be fully discussed later but you need to establish a to-do list now.

Size

During the initial planning stages you should determine how many family members you're inviting to the reunion. This can be as few as the immediate family or may go back several generations . Keep the crowd size manageable for the activities you'd like to plan. When tracing your family, work slowly and thoroughly back through each generation. The worst mistake you could make would be to exclude someone through hasty decision making.

Date

Determine early in the planning what time of year and what time of day works best for your family reunion. Once these decisions are made, select a theme and get into the more minute details.

Theme

Choosing a theme is probably the biggest and most controversial decision of the event. Everyone seems to have very specific ideas regarding what constitutes the perfect family reunion. The best advice for this category is to be flexible and listen to all ideas, especially from people who have attended successful reunions in the past.

GUEST OF HONOR

Before choosing a guest of honor, tell the person of your intentions. You'll find yourself in an awkward position if the invitations are issued and the intended guest of honor doesn't want the attention.

COSTS

There are two sets of costs associated with a family reunion. The first are the costs of setting up the event which include phone bills, invitations, postage, poster board, transportation, and deposits. Money spent by family members attending the reunion must be considered, too. These include, but are not limited to food, entertainment, T-shirts, and transportation. Set up logs at the beginning of the planning process to track all money spent (see Appendix).

HAVING FUN

At some point, you're bound to ask yourself why you bothered getting involved in planning the reunion. This is completely understandable. Don't be too hard on yourself when it happens.

On the other hand, if your goal is to have fun planning a party, to gather everyone together to celebrate being a member of the "Tomich" family, or learn more about your family history, you'll certainly feel successful. If you run into a roadblock, compare the reunion planning to completing a puzzle. Each task completed brings you closer to a successful family reunion.

Set specific deadlines for completing projects such as compiling names, sending invitations, booking the site, or purchasing the prizes for the children's games. You'll enjoy a sense of satisfaction as you see the tasks completed.

You may want to motivate yourself and your committee with little rewards at the completion of major projects. These rewards could be as minor as extra dessert portions to the extravagance of giving yourself a day off from reunion planning.

TIMING

Now that the planning team has been assembled, it's time to schedule the reunion. Since everyone on the committee will be excited to get started, take advantage of this enthusiasm and quickly pick the date. Create interest within the family by hinting there is a reunion in the works, you just don't have enough information available at this time to provide details.

CHOOSING THE DATE

When planning any sort of party or event, you try to pick the right date so everyone you've invited will be able to attend. No matter how far in advance you do your planning, however, some people will have made previous commitments. Also, there will always be last-minute cancellations. As a general rule, you can lower the guest count by five percent because of these last-minute changes.

Once you make a decision on the date, quickly notify everyone on the guest list. If you receive too many regrets, your first inclination may be to reschedule the reunion. Changing the date only complicates matters by confusing those who have now made plans based on the original invitation. Pick the date and issue invitations with as much advance notice as possible and don't make any changes in the date.

KEEP THE DATE FIRM

If some family members call and let you know they won't be attending the reunion, don't panic. Express your disappointment that they're unable to join the festivities, but don't give any indication the plans can or will be changed. You may be disappointed, but try to understand that their non-attendance is not a personal rejection. Not everyone is comfortable saying they aren't interested in events such as family reunions, so don't push for a reason if none is offered.

Some people may be upset if they are unable to convince you to change the date of the reunion. Be prepared to deal with complaints concerning your inflexibility or unwillingness to cooperate. When accepting regrets, do so in a positive way. Point out how much you'll miss them, but remind them a date had to be selected.

SUMMER DATES

Most family reunions are traditionally planned for the summer months. The weather is better for both the reunion and traveling to the reunion, children are out of school, and people are more inclined to take vacations in the summer.

Summer reunion planners have the advantage of being able to work with three long holiday weekends. Summer holidays have traditionally been used as excuses (or reasons) to have a party. People naturally tend to gather when they are able to take advantage of three day weekends. The extra day allows time for an additional activity without breaking into weekend routines. Take advantage of this and plan your reunion when people are already expecting a party of some sort.

A Memorial Day reunion could begin with a presentation involving your family history listing all of your ancestors who died in military or public safety service. Incorporate the meaning of the holiday into your reunion and make it special for your family. You may even want to plan a religious service on this day if your family is so inclined.

On the Fourth of July, consider sites near public firework displays so you can enjoy the viewing at no extra cost to your family. Encourage the children to make a Statue of Liberty costume. This can be done ahead of time or planned as a reunion day activity. For an appropriate prize, give each child who participates a picture book about the statue.

If the party is scheduled on Labor Day weekend, stick to a *working people* theme. Request that all of your relatives bring a photograph taken of them at work. This is a great conversation starter. Give out prizes for the most unusual job, the longest time at the same job, the funniest job, or the most dangerous occupation. Give pens inscribed with the family reunion date as prizes.

Crowds are a possibility on holiday weekends, but that shouldn't stop you from taking advantage of an ideal time for the reunion. Just be aware that places may tend to be more crowded than usual because so many people have a similar idea. Most parks or recreation areas will take reservations and set aside an area for you to conduct your festivities, so call and reserve your site as soon as possible.

WINTER DATES

A winter reunion almost needs to be planned around Thanksgiving, Christmas, or Chanukah. Because most people devote so much time and energy to the traditional celebration of the above holidays, there's little desire to put in the effort to plan or attend another major event during the winter months.

The Thanksgiving holiday has the advantage of being a four day weekend for most people. The nature of this holiday makes people plan celebrations with family rather than friends so it's a very appropriate time for a reunion. Christmas or Chanukah is also a time when family traditions abound. One advantage of planning a reunion for this time of year is that the themes and decorations are predetermined. A holiday reunion may also appeal to those who spend quite a bit of time paying visits to various relatives. This would enable all the visiting to be done at one time.

There are two other types of winter reunions that are guaranteed to interest your family. Try celebrating the event in a warm weather state. If you are lucky enough to have relatives in these locations, by all means take advantage of their hospitality, their area, and their weather. Children and adults alike will look forward to a little time in a warm climate. Plan as many reunion events as possible around a sunshine theme to brighten the spirits of the snowbound relatives. In the weeks prior to the reunion, send photocopied articles from the local paper that mention great weather to tantalize the guests.

Or, if a warm climate is out of the question, plan the reunion at a hotel or motel with an indoor pool and jacuzzi. Whether for a day or over the weekend, this will appeal to the need for a break from the winter snow shovelling routine. Carry out the sunshine theme by taking advantage of the facilities for your activities. Use the pool for races, the hotel game room for *hot* video competitions, and the dining room for a "Summer in Paradise" formal dinner.

Even if the reunion is scheduled indoors, remember people still have to get there. It's a good idea to schedule major activities sometime after the first hour to allow for late arrivals.

SPECIAL OCCASIONS

A family reunion can also be organized around special occasion days. Take advantage of a special birthday or anniversary and incorporate it into the party theme. Reunions have also been successfully planned around a wedding. It works perfectly to have an *adult only* wedding one day and gather all generations the next.

If you are planning the reunion to coincide with another occasion, discuss your plans with the person or persons celebrating their special event. Get their permission to share the limelight. In the case of planning the reunion around a wedding, the reunion needs to be held after, not before, the couple's big day.

Other occasions you might consider planning around the reunion include christenings, first communions, bar or bat mitzvahs, graduations, and house warmings.

SPORTING EVENTS

Many of your guests might prefer not to attend a family function if they are interested in a major sporting event which may conflict with the reunion. The key to attracting this segment of the family is to appeal to their interests. Consider having the reunion the day before or the day after a major sporting event. Some events near the reunion location could include the Super Bowl, an auto race, or the All-Star game. If you do your homework and plan smartly, the sport enthusiast who doesn't live near the major event will be begging to come to the reunion.

Include an order form to the box office where the event will be held with the invitations. Those attending the above activities can then make their own arrangements, without involving the reunion planners. Help out-of-town relatives with suggestions, but let them make their own decisions on how they plan to enjoy themselves during non-reunion time.

The Importance of a Date

There is more involved to scheduling the reunion than picking up a calendar and selecting a date. Be thoughtful in your selection since you want as large a turnout as possible. Once the date is firm, you can begin issuing the invitations.

4

CONTACT THE RELATIVES

*Y*ou can't have a reunion without relatives. Finding family members may be a challenge, but once everyone is together your efforts will have proven worthwhile. After the first reunion, planners will have a much easier time since there will be a mailing list available.

ASK, ASK, ASK

You have to find your family before you can invite them (See Appendix). This means a complete search. Start with the previous generation when you begin looking for relatives. If your parents are alive, question them first. If not, contact an aunt or uncle. Ask about their parents and grandparents, as well as the brothers and sisters of their parents and grandparents. You'll need to know the married name of any women family members who may have changed their name after marriage. Hopefully, the conversations with your immediate relatives will give you enough information to get started in your search.

Next, make a decision on how many generations to include in your reunion. Remember, the further back you go, the larger the crowd. This may or may not be a concern, depending on the type of reunion you choose. You don't want more people attending than you can accommodate.

While you are investigating your branch, enlist the help of family members in other branches to do the same. Announce a special award for the family branch that finds the most relatives. The perfect prize would be a small address book with the reunion date imprinted on the front. You may also want to give a prize to the relative who tracks down the person who has been *lost* the longest. A gift certificate for long distance phone calls would be an appreciated and appropriate prize.

After all branches have turned in the names of their family members, swap lists and double check them for completeness. You may be surprised by the number of relatives you have!

GENEALOGY CHART

If anyone in your family has organized a genealogy chart, you'll be able to quickly and easily know who to invite to the reunion. Genealogy, which is the study of one's family history, is a common hobby so check with your relatives to see if it's been done.

If your family has not begun the process of tracing its roots, you may want to contact the National Genealogical Society for help and direction. Write or call:

National Genealogical Society
4527 17th Street, North
Arlington, VA 22207-2399
(703) 525-0050

USE THE COMPUTER

If your computer has communications softwear, you may want to try the genealogical bulletin boards to find your relatives. Compuserve, America Online, Prodigy, and GEnie have genealogy bulletin board areas.

The National Genealogical Society also includes information for the computer interest group as part of their quarterly newsletter.

ESTABLISH A MAILING LIST

Regardless of how the family members are to be contacted, a data bank should be established with all the pertinent information on each person. Include each person's name, address, spouse's name, children, and phone number. Keep a copy of this information in a notebook at the reunion so it can be updated if necessary.

FAMILY BRANCH NAME _____

FAMILY NAME _____

Name _____
Address _____
_____
City _____
State _____Zip _____
Spouse _____
Children _____
_____
Phone Number ( ) _____

WORD OF MOUTH

It may be tempting to invite people to the reunion on an informal, haphazard basis. Though verbal invitations may appear to be an acceptable method of inviting family members, it's likely to cause serious problems in organizing activities and menus. The planning committee (or individual) will have no idea how many people have been invited and who plans to attend.

Without something in writing, most people are not sure how serious you are about a party. There's always the fear you'll change your mind and not inform them. Finally, people are less inclined to feel badly if they are unable to attend a casual party because they often feel that their presence won't be missed.

Another problem with word of mouth invitations is that details get lost in the translation as they are passed from one person to the next. Like the old game of telephone, the original time, date, and theme are likely to be totally mixed up by the time the invitation reaches the tenth person.

An additional drawback of a word of mouth invitation is that many people don't write down the information as it's given to them. Either it's forgotten, or they call you later to verify everything they were told. Save yourself the aggravation and don't consider notifying relatives of a reunion in this manner.

By Telephone

Though a telephone invitation may also appear to be an easy solution, it has many drawbacks. You may be the most organized person in the world, but other people don't necessarily write things down or keep an up-to-date calendar of events. When you call months in advance to notify relatives of the reunion, they are unlikely to remember all the details without some form of reminder.

Usually there is a great deal of information to be exchanged. The call must include information on when, where, time, directions, theme, guest of honor, what they need to bring, and how to dress. The average person is so busy writing down information they hardly have time to think of questions they might want answered.

Trying to contact relatives via the phone often results in a game of telephone tag. Answering machines are of some help in delivering a message, but are no substitute to direct communication.

If you decide to notify by phone, solicit a member from each branch to make the phone calls to their family. They probably speak with these family members regularly. Remind everyone making calls to log them and keep notes on the information they receive. This will be helpful in determining both time and cost factors of planning the reunion(See Appendix).

By Letter

People receive so few personal letters they have become a pleasant surprise. Anyone opening their mailbox and finding a hand addressed letter will give it their full attention.

Select stationery which reflects the theme of the reunion. Choose white or cream for a formal party, primary colors for a barbecue, or red and green for the holidays. Remember, you want to get attention immediately so choose paper that says, "Look at me!"

Letters should be handwritten rather than typed. An acceptable compromise would be to photocopy a handwritten letter onto your colorful paper. List all pertinent information in the letter making it informative in addition to being chatty.

BY INVITATION

A simple invitation that lists the basic information needed by your relatives is often the best kind. There is no need for wordiness to get your message across. Keep the invitation as uncluttered as possible (see Appendix).

A basic invitation will cover date, location (including directions), time, theme, guest of honor, anything the guest should bring, and a stamped self-addressed envelope or telephone number for responses. Keeping the invitation simple doesn't mean you can't do it with flair. Here are a few examples of fun ways to present the invitation:

- Write the invitation on the back of a photograph of the reunion site.
- Make a video showing current family members and old photographs, closing with the specifics of the family reunion.
- Deliver the invitation with a seasonal bouquet.
- Fill the envelope with sparkly confetti.
- Send the invitation over the fax machine.

CHILDREN CAN HELP

Children enjoy helping out and often come up with very creative ideas. Allow a seven to ten year old to help design the invitations. After they are printed, provide a box of crayons and let them add the colorful touches (See Appendix). Most people think drawings by children are cute.

During the upcoming reunion, one activity that can be planned for children is designing invitations. Display all the drawings and take a vote for the best one. The chosen design will be used as the official invitation for the next reunion. Make sure every child signs their handiwork so credit can be given where it's due.

PREPRINTED INVITATIONS

At this time, there isn't a line of preprinted invitations on the market for family reunions. When they do become available, make sure all the information you need to communicate is on the invitation before you make your purchase. Every reunion planner needs information specific to their family so preprinted invitations may not be the best option.

RSVP

A major cause of misunderstanding between those planning an event and those receiving an invitation is the meaning of the letters RSVP at the bottom of the invitation. Since they do not mean the same thing to every person, it's better for you to spell out exactly what you want the invited person to do. Ask them to respond if they are attending, to respond if they aren't attending, or to respond either way—just make sure to respond. This can tactfully be worded in the following manner, "Let us know whether or not you will be attending so we can plan accordingly." Save later aggravation by being specific in your requests to your relatives during the planning stages.

THE ANSWERING MACHINE

A convenient way to receive the replies is to use an answering machine. This allows those responding the opportunity to call at their convenience. Here is an ideal message for the answering machine:

> Thank you for calling this machine to give your response for the "Compton" family reunion. At the tone, leave your name, phone number (in case further contact is necessary), whether or not you will be attending, how many will be attending, ages of the children attending (to set up games at the reunion), and any way you are available to assist at the reunion.

When sending out invitations, inform everyone they will be responding to an answering machine. Some people are uncomfortable talking to a machine but will do so if forewarned. Also, let them know the exact questions the machine will be asking. This will enable them to prepare their answers and not become tongue-tied and omit important information. Consider giving an alternate phone number for those who refuse to speak to a machine.

ENCOURAGING A RESPONSE

Set a date for the guests to notify you as to whether or not they'll be attending. This will allow you to establish an accurate head count and plan the activities on reunion day accordingly. Though not a one hundred percent guaranteed, written in stone number, you'll at least have a general idea of your crowd size and their ages.

When talking to family members as they respond to the invitation, inquire about relatives who haven't replied. Don't accept second hand information as their reply, but at least verify their invitation was received.

Some family members won't reply to the first request. They will need a follow-up call or a postcard to motivate them. Provide a second or third opportunity to reply before giving up on anyone.

To encourage a quick response, offer a reward for the first phone RSVP as well as the earliest postmark on a written reply. Since these people were prompt in their feedback, give them public recognition at the reunion. A personal phone book for them to write down newly found family members is a good thank you. Present a calendar for the following year to the relative who is last to respond (regardless of the excuse) to help them get organized.

TRACKING RESPONSES

Establish a method of keeping track of invitations sent and the responses received. A form was designed to help you with this (see Appendix). It covers all the information needed to track the responses.

You will notice spaces to enter the dates of follow-up contacts. This helps keep track of those who aren't prompt in their response. It's a good idea to enter the follow-up dates in a different colored pen than the one you originally used so your attention is drawn to those relatives.

When making your log, make sure there is a response column for every question you asked. By setting up your log in an efficient manner, you'll be able to tell at a glance the status of every family member.

YOU'VE DONE WELL

Now that you've found your relatives and issued invitations, you've accomplished a major step toward having a successful reunion. A sizable crowd allows for more activities, games, and conversations. Introducing newly discovered relatives to those already acquainted family members will be your reward on reunion day.

EXPENSES

*P*lanning a family reunion does not require a large budget. With a bit of creativity and attention to costs, you can make the process relatively painless. Keep good records, so future reunion planners have a ready made cost-cutting guide

POSTAGE

The best way to notify relatives of the upcoming reunion is through the mail. Avoid having to send information more than once by including everything needed in one packet. Sending information in a piecemeal manner substantially increases the amount of money you spend on postage. With the invitation include directions, a biography sheet, the response postcard (or a self-addressed, stamped envelope), and a list of everything guests should bring on reunion day.

A self-addressed, stamped envelope is crucial if you want relatives to reply via the mail. Don't look at this as an expense, but rather a necessity. People are more likely to respond if you make it easy for them to do so. To some relatives just finding an envelope to send a response is a challenge. Since you are planning to call each person that doesn't reply, including the self-addressed, stamped envelope for their convenience will reduce the number of follow-up calls you'll have to make later.

PAPER

Put as much information on as little paper as possible. The back of the invitation is the ideal place to put directions to the reunion. Once this is done, all information will be on the same piece of paper and the directions are less likely to be misplaced.

Make it easy for relatives to respond by eliminating the need to do much writing. Have little spaces that can be checked. The example below can be used for almost any theme.

The _____ family _____ (will) _____ (will not) be attending the family reunion on July 4th. There will be _____ adults, _____ children five and under, _____ children six thru twelve, and_____ teenagers attending.

I plan to bring _____ for the meal (enough for a dozen people). Also, I will help out the day of the reunion:

_____ Yes _____ No

PLEASE RETURN BY JUNE 10TH. THANK YOU!

This preprinted card gives you all the information you need regarding head count, age group breakdown, food items being brought, and the willingness to help out on the reunion day. It's also extremely simple for the respondent.

TELEPHONE

Telephone bills begin the day you think up the idea and call your mother or sister to ask their opinion on the subject. Telephone bills stop a week after the reunion has ended and you've matched up the leftover clothing with the departed relatives. There's a long time period in between and it's essential to use a telephone log to track these costs (see Appendix). It's important to be able to tell future reunion planners of all money spent during the organizational phase.

Take advantage of the experts at the telephone company by calling and asking questions. Be sure to contact both the local telephone company and your long distance carrier (their numbers are on the first page of your telephone bill) to ask the following questions:

> What time of the day and what day of the week are rates lowest?
> How many miles away can I call without getting into long distance charges?
> Can I temporarily change my service to utilize a less expensive plan while organizing this reunion?

Time spent making these calls now will save money later.

The best time to contact relatives regarding the reunion is when the person you are calling is home and awake. Calling older people late in the evening, even if the rates are lower, is a bad idea. People who go to bed early don't appreciate being awakened just to chat. Another reason not to call too late in the evening is that almost everyone associates late night calls with emergencies. No one is receptive to discussing a party after being frightened by the telephone.

Try to schedule the call when you know your relatives are home, but avoid calling at mealtime. If they aren't home and the call is picked up by an answering machine, you will be charged for a one minute call. Use the time to leave the following message:

> "This is _____ calling regarding the _____
> family reunion scheduled for _____. Please call me back
> at ___*(phone number)*___ and let me know whether or not you will
> be attending, ages of the children attending, the food item you are bringing, and if you plan to help out at the party. Please call between
> ___*(time)*___ ___*(day)*___ or ___*(day)*___."

These are your relatives so you're going to have to decide whether or not you'll place collect calls to long distance family members. As a rule, it's not advisable to call collect for any reason. If you've gotten to the point of thinking this might not be a bad idea (you've called them repeatedly with no response), just give up. There is no reason to continuously pursue anyone. You may decide you want to make two calls or ten calls, but don't drive yourself crazy over lack of response.

Rental Fees and Deposits

Some places you may be considering for the reunion site will require a cash outlay in the form of rental money or a reservation fee. In addition to the rent, a deposit is often paid to cover any damage caused to the building itself. This deposit money is returned at the end of the rental period if all conditions of the agreement are met.

Make sure you understand what conditions must be met for getting your deposit refunded. Some facilities provide the cleanup crew—you just need to leave the walls standing. Others require a complete cleanup that includes scrubbing the floors. Before signing a rental contract, ask questions. When all your questions have been answered, read and reread the contract BEFORE signing it to verify what you have verbally agreed to is actually what the contract spells out. You are legally responsible for what the contract states, not what was discussed.

Your Budget

If money is a major concern and coming up with a deposit is difficult, find a relative who will host the event at their home. Depending on the size of the home and surrounding property, you may have to scale back the number of activities or guests, but don't let costs keep you from having the reunion.

Another option for eliminating or reducing up-front costs to the planner is to choose a venue such as a cruise where the money is paid directly to a third party by each attendee. You may be the person who is responsible for taking the deposit and final payment checks to the travel agent organizing your reunion, but you won't be responsible for any more than your share. Since cruise lines have a date when the deposits are due, you will be able to have an accurate total on that day of the size of your reunion crowd.

Running Errands

Every time you get into the car to go to the post office, stationery store, committee meeting, or site scouting trip, transportation expenses are mounting. All of these trips may be necessary, but try to consolidate them. Organize yourself so that each time you go out the door you have at least two stops planned. Again, make sure these errands are tracked on your expense log.

Before you get into the car to run reunion related errands, make a few telephone calls. Keep a copy of both the Yellow Pages and your local business-to-business telephone directory handy and call a few places to compare prices. Often the cost of an item varies from store to store.

ASK FOR DISCOUNTS

Don't be shy! When purchasing a large quantity of an item, ask for a discount. Even grocery stores may give discounts if you purchase a full case, so don't be afraid to ask. The worst they can tell you is no. A potential ten or twenty percent saving is worth the risk of hearing discounts aren't given.

Shop warehouse stores, discount outlets, and surplus stores. Use your creativity and shop at places which have savings built in their image. Know the cost at a full price store so you can judge if it's really a better deal. Purchase large quantities only if you need a lot of the item.

If you are booking a hotel or cruise reunion, and a certain number of rooms are paid for, ask about a free accommodation for yourself. This information isn't public knowledge so you'll have to ask. If you're booking over twenty spaces, don't hesitate to inquire.

RECOVER PLANNING EXPENSES

Can the planner recoup any expenses? This is a valid question, but you probably won't like the answer. In some circumstances you may be able to get back the money you've spent, but it's highly unlikely. Here are a few suggestions reimburse yourself for money spent on the reunion.

Estimate the expenses and ask for a proportional amount from each family unit attending the reunion. This can be done by asking that the money be included with a mailed response or it can be brought along on the day of the reunion. Again, you have to know how your family is going to react to being asked for money. They may include their check with a smile or they may view you as a petty individual to even suggest having your expenses reimbursed.

You can set out a large, nicely decorated donation jar for voluntary contributions. This jar should be located at the check-in point or another visible spot. Divide the money in the jar at the end of the day among all those who had out-of-pocket expenses.

Have family members bring homemade items to auction off. The items to be auctioned can include jellies and jams, Christmas ornaments, bird houses, kitchen towels (with the family name on them), or clothing. Sell the item to the highest bidder and use the money to pay for reunion expenses. This sale at the reunion can become a tradition and relatives will soon be making special items throughout the year to contribute to the auction.

The best attitude to have regarding expenses for the family reunion is to view the whole process as a labor of love. If you start adding up the time and money spent, you'll soon dislike all your relatives. You'll be a happier person if you have a *money is not an object* attitude, especially if the planning is done at a reasonable cost.

TRAVEL EXPENSES

Though the reunion planners have the bulk of the expenses, relatives traveling from out of the area will also have expenses. These include gasoline, meals, lodging, entertainment, and miscellaneous expenses. Some of these costs can be reduced if people double up on car transportation or welcome out-of-town relatives into their homes. If long distance relatives decline your reunion invitation, be understanding that the expenses of attending may just be too much for their pocketbook this year.

BALANCE WANTS AND THE BUDGET

The chief goal of a family reunion is to have a good time. This can mean different things to different people. A large family that has a lot of young children would probably do better outdoors with many activities to keep them occupied. A group that has a large number of pre-teens and teens would consider a disk jockey or music mandatory. Middle aged attendees are probably willing to pay a little extra money for more convenience and less work. Elderly relatives can't be expected to sit outdoors on the ground all day. The challenge is to balance the wants of every age group with the budget available.

Parents are always looking for inexpensive activities their children enjoy. Make it fun for the kids; they will bring their parents back the following year. Not everyone will be happy if they feel there are not enough activities scheduled for their age group, but making the reunion fun and convenient to the grandparents and children will improve your chances of a good turnout.

FUN IS FREE

A lot of fun to be had on reunion day doesn't cost a dime. Scrapbooks can be assembled and shown, a story on how the family name originated can be told, children can draw pictures of each other on paper recycled from the office, or have their face painted, and a game of volleyball can be played. Don't lose sight of the fact that most of the expenses are incurred before the reunion. On the day of the party, fun can be free.

LOCATION

*C*hoosing the right location is among the most important decisions you'll make in planning the reunion. You can use the site to enhance the theme and entice guests to attend. There are many options available for different, unusual, and exciting locations. You can have it in your home, a nearby park, a local restaurant, or a centrally located facility. You can even plan a family vacation in an exotic locale.

CHOOSING THE LOCATION

A locale convenient to the planner isn't necessarily convenient to the rest of the relatives. However, as the organizer, you can plan the reunion for wherever you want. There's nothing wrong with planning the reunion at your house or in your neighborhood. Since you've done all the pre-party work, you're entitled to a little convenience on reunion day!

While looking for a central location, spend some time getting the feel of the area. Plan time for lunching at a local restaurant, wandering through the center of town, and speaking with local merchants. You'll enjoy getting the flavor of the community. In the end, you are likely to decide on an area central to all relatives. People are more likely to show up if they don't have to travel far.

If the theme is interesting enough, family members will travel long distances to attend. In this case, you can plan the reunion in a place that's inconvenient for everyone and still have a good turnout. Remember, this only works if you can come up with an exciting theme. Try these themes to draw your crowd:

- A day at Disneyland
- Grandma's 90th birthday party
- Family member in best physical shape
- Reunion takes place the day after Uncle Jim's wedding
- Family heritage day with everyone's favorite food

Once you have determined where the reunion will be held, incorporate the setting into the theme. For outdoor reunions, consider the land, water, buildings, shade trees, and weather when picking your theme. When looking at the site, open your mind to it's possibilities. Take advantage of the slope of the hills for sack races, the flat spaces for ball games, and the shady areas for food storage and conversation.

For indoor reunions, a raised area can double as seating for the guest of honor and a stage for the family talent show. A poster can be displayed on the wall for part of the reunion, and later taken down so the wall can become a screen for watching a video. A large coat room could easily become the children's nap area. Indoor reunions can also be chosen to accommodate a dance floor and a bandstand.

WORKING WITH THE WEATHER

Remember, it always rains on an outdoor party if you don't have a back-up plan. Unless the reunion is scheduled in Southern California during the middle of July, don't expect the weather to cooperate. Since you can't change the weather, be prepared to change your plans at a moments notice or, if necessary, in the middle of the event. If the rains begin during the reunion, know in advance how long you're willing to wait out the showers before moving inside.

Most parks have a shelter or lean-to on the grounds. Do whatever is necessary to get that spot. While some parks operate on a first-come first-served basis, others require reservations and deposits. Find out early what procedures need to be followed to insure getting this choice location. If weather forces you into the lean-to, use this time for the talent show, stories by older family members remembering their youth, or the guest of honor tribute. Since the possibility of rain was considered, the pace of the reunion won't slow down. The party will just move in a different direction.

Another alternative is to arrange the use of a nearby home in case of inclement weather. Though this will change the reunion activities, at least the day won't be a total loss. You can tell scary stories in the basement, play board games, have a sing-a-long, or spread blankets on the floor and continue the picnic. If you're perky and upbeat about the change in agenda, the guests will be too,

If the weather is bad the morning of the reunion and you're changing the location, you can notify your relatives in a variety of ways. Have someone answering the response number (or hook up an answering machine) to give directions to the new site. Initiate contact to those attending and inform them of the new plans. For those who took the chance of showing up regardless of the weather, you'll need someone standing in the rain at the original site passing out flyers with directions to the new location. Try to modify plans and notify relatives before they get the idea that the reunion has been cancelled and they should spend the day in bed.

If all or most of the guests live in the area and it's raining the day of the reunion, consider rescheduling the party. Contact the relatives who sent a positive response and inform them of the new date. Recognize that people who were available on the original date may have commitments on the rescheduled one.

OTHER OUTDOOR CONSIDERATIONS

When picking a location for an outdoor reunion there are two major issues in addition to the weather to consider. These are bathroom facilities and the availability of water. The facilities should be reasonably close, but not too close, to the central gathering area. Remember, children wait until the last minute so make sure the rest room facilities are convenient.

If water is not available throughout the grounds, you'll need to bring it with you. Keep a supply of water near the game areas, ball fields, eating areas, and anywhere fires are built. Make sure there is enough water available to fill water balloons because the activity will surely come up during the day. There is nothing more fun than water balloon toss and eventually water fights on a hot summer day!

ALTERNATIVES TO A PICNIC

Though most people think of a family reunion as an outdoor picnic, this doesn't have to be the case. If the crowd is older, you may want to consider a restaurant location and organize a dinner dance. This could be a gala, first class affair, rather than the traditional barbecue. Tailor your location and theme so it is appropriate for your age groups.

Choosing an alternative location rather than a local park or restaurant is becoming increasingly popular. A good example of this is a cruise. Cruise lines make it convenient for the planner because they eliminate all the work except for the invitations. This type of reunion would have to be planned a few years in advance so potential guests would have time to save for the trip.

Another popular, and less expensive, location is a hotel or motel. This is especially attractive as a place families can gather in the winter months when the weather outdoors is miserable. It is enjoyable to take advantage of the pool, jacuzzi, game room, cable television, nightclub, and restaurant without having to leave the location. Most of the larger chains have discounted rates on the weekend, and a few of them allow children to share a room with an adult at no additional charge.

CONSIDER DISABILITY NEEDS

When scouting for a location, take into consideration that some of your relatives may have a disability. Pay attention to wheelchair access in both the general environment and the rest room facilities. Make sure there are low curbs and ramps.

Some of your elderly relatives may be using a cane or walker. They may need assistance at various times during the reunion, so have physically strong people available to provide help if necessary. Since you may not know all the people attending, it's best to assume there's at least one with a handicap. Everyone will have a good time if you have the foresight to examine the location for possible problems.

LOCATION CHECKLIST

A list of location considerations will make your decision easier and efficient.

On-site Inspection

_____	Is it easy to find?
_____	Is there adequate parking?
_____	Is there enough space for all planned activities?
_____	Is the setting appropriate for many different activities?
_____	Is cooking permitted? Do they have barbecue pits?
_____	How many bathrooms are available? How close are the bathrooms? How clean are the bathrooms?
_____	How many water fountains are available? Are they convenient to all the areas we will be using?
_____	Is there enough shade during all times of the day?
_____	Is the layout appropriate for handicapped relatives?

Legal Matters

_____	How much is the rental fee?
_____	How much is the security deposit?
_____	When is the security deposit returned?
_____	How clean do we have to leave the site?
_____	How do we reserve the site we want?
_____	How far in advance do we reserve the site we want?
_____	How do we move strangers who don't know the park space is reserved off the site? (This is an important issue since most parties are on weekends when the rental agent is gone!)
_____	How late into the evening can we use the facility?
_____	Are alcoholic beverages allowed at the site?
_____	What are the emergency numbers for this location?

fire_____

police_____

poison control_____

hospital_____

EMERGENCIES

Post a notice (See example on page 52) at the reunion site listing the major cross streets of your location as well as specific directions from those streets to where your group is located. List landmarks or buildings that help identify where you are.

Include directions to the nearest hospital. Make these directions easy to follow by using right and left rather than the compass directions of north, south, east, and west. This makes it easier for someone unfamiliar with the area to get to emergency facilities.

Emergency numbers such as fire, police, paramedic, and poison control need to be listed. These numbers should be posted where food is being cooked, in the rest rooms, and at the entrance.

Finally, on your posted notice write down the number of the nearest phone. Make sure this phone is close to your group so it gets answered whenever it rings. With today's technology, you may want to list the portable cellular phone number of one of the guests. This insures all incoming and outgoing calls will get a response.

SENIOR FAMILY REUNION

We are at Gallup Park in Ann Arbor.
Exit Geddes Road West off of US 23

The park entrance is 2.7 miles down Geddes (just past Huron Parkway).
There is a large pavilion visible from the road as well as a
"Senior Family Reunion"
sign posted.

Our phone number in the park _____

Fire/Emergency number is 911

Poison control _____

Hospital Telephone Number is _____

The nearest hospital is University of Michigan Hospital. Turn **left** out of the park back on to Geddes Road. This road changes names to Fuller Road near the Veteran Administration Hospital. When you come to the first stop sign, turn **left**—this is still Fuller Road. The hospital is approximately two miles down the road on the **left**.

THE IMPORTANCE OF LOCATION

The reunion can be planned as a once-in-a-lifetime vacation or it can be handled on a shoestring budget. Because different age groups have different needs, choose the location carefully before notifying the relatives. Remember that children need lots of space and constant entertainment, elderly people need comfort, and teenagers would prefer to be anywhere else!

FAMILY RELATIONSHIPS

*T*he number one rule of family reunions is not to make attendance decisions for anyone other than yourself. Invite everyone, no matter who they aren't speaking to, or how difficult they may be. You'll be surprised how many people are prepared to forget arguments and personal dislikes rather than risk being excluded.

If Aunt Donna suggests eliminating relatives she doesn't like from the guest list, turn a deaf ear. Once the planners start getting involved with family conflicts, trouble begins. Before anyone knows what's happening, it's time to choose sides and you've become part of a bigger problem. Cajole, humor, or ignore a quarrelsome relative, but DO NOT give in to their demands or threats.

DEALING WITH FEUDS

You won't necessarily know who is on bad terms with their relatives. While you need to stay out of the middle of family conflicts, you'll have to find out what's going on in other branches. The organizers need to know of these problems so they can be on the lookout to maintain peace. And remember, the feud is a consequence of their behavior, not yours. You don't need (or want) to take responsibility for resolving conflicts.

If a committee is involved with the planning, they'll be able to investigate who is at odds by discussing the subject during a meeting. Otherwise, be direct and ask. This information can be discovered by questioning relatives as they call to confirm attendance. It may also be volunteered by those involved in the disagreements.

If a relative questions the attendance of another family member, find out why. It may be because they haven't seen them for a while. On the other hand, they may be requesting this information because they don't care to spend time together.

When informed of feuds, respect the feelings of those involved. Don't use the reunion as a public forum to try and force them to reconcile. It isn't necessary to fix the situation or make them like each other. If you make them feel guilty because they're involved in a disagreement, they may decide against attending.

Most people aren't going to advertise the fact that they're a participant in a feud. Respect their privacy. Only become involved if you notice one member of a feud trying to stir up trouble by discussing the problem with every relative they encounter. At that point, step in and insist the topic not be discussed.

KEEPING EVERYONE BUSY

One way to keep feuding family members apart is to make sure options are available as to where each person can physically locate. Reduce the possibility of fighting by separating relatives who don't get along. As the planner, you can make sure there are plenty of available places for eating, games, conversation, and just escaping.

The feuding relatives may enjoy competing against each each other by joining volleyball or tug-o-war teams. There's nothing like some honest competition to dilute hostilities.

Assign responsibility to family members you know are involved in a feud. Make sure the assigned project will show them in a positive light. If the disagreement is common knowledge, seeing the person as helpful and cooperative may change a few opinions. A relative who is best known as never on time may be excellent with children if given the opportunity to umpire the baseball game. Find a new, positive trait in a feuding relative—don't reinforce negative, and possibly outdated, stereotypes.

There is the chance that no matter how much effort is exerted to keep some relatives apart, they'll try to use the reunion as the place to settle their differences. This puts you in the touchy position of giving them the space they need for their confrontation but keeping their personal issues from becoming the focal point of the reunion.

At the first sign of a possible confrontation, encourage the people involved to temporarily remove themselves from the gathering. Remind them that the reunion is for everyone and the entire family may not be interested in a discussion of their problems.

Take a little time during the reunion and compliment the people involved in feuds for ignoring their personal feelings for the good of the whole family. Let Aunt Karen know you're aware of her disagreement with Uncle Bryan, and tell her she's doing an outstanding job of maintaining a good attitude. A little positive reinforcement goes a long way. People like to receive compliments—especially if they're doing something which is difficult for them.

REGRETS CAUSED BY DISAGREEMENTS

There may be some feuds so long-standing and bitter that the parties involved are unable or unwilling to face each other. Rather than risk ruining the reunion, one of the relatives may decline to attend if the other is present. If this happens, inform the relative who has chosen not to attend various ways they can avoid the other family member.

Even after your pep talk, an individual involved in a feud may be uncomfortable attending the reunion. Graciously accept the news they won't be at the party. Without comment, note the reason the invitation was declined in case the other party to the disagreement is unable to attend. If that should occur, place a call to the first relative who declined and see if they are now interested in attending. And remember: it's not necessary for you to share their conflict.

DIFFICULT RELATIVES

You may have family members at the reunion who aren't involved in feuds, but are difficult all the same. These are the people who empty a room by walking into it. They are opinionated, loud, and offensive to everyone. Unfortunately, they are also your relatives and have a right to be at the reunion!

You'll probably have to schedule people to sit with them at various points during the day if they are to have any interaction at all. Enlist the relatives you know best to sit with them at specific times. Children are also useful in entertaining this type of personality. Encourage cousin Scott to review his baseball card collection or Lousie to discuss school activities as a form of diversion.

DISCIPLINING CHILDREN

When you get children together you'll have to allow time for them to work out the difficulties of playing with each other. Every parent has a different standard for what they consider acceptable behavior for their child. While one parent may discipline their child over an incident, another parent may look away and say nothing. ONLY DISCIPLINE YOUR OWN CHILD!!! A sure way to start the next major family feud is to have relatives tell each other how to raise their children. If you feel a child is behaving inappropriately to you or your child, and the parent is not reacting to the situation, walk away.

Kids will be kids, but there is a point where playing can turn into hurting. Older children trying to play with babies may become rough without realizing it. Contact sports can turn violent when players try to get even with each other. Make sure you keep an eye on **your** children to determine they aren't the cause of these types of problems.

SUPERVISING CHILDREN

Before the reunion begins, set up a log for each area that requires adult supervision. Divide the log into hour segments listing the adult in charge. Solicit volunteers or assign the supervision tasks to those family members with children. This assures the playgrounds, ball fields, and eating areas have someone accepting responsibility at all times. Keep the log handy, so everyone knows when their hour of responsibility begins and ends. Make separate lists for each monitored area.

The key to having children who are happy and under control is proper supervision. Parents should know where their children are at all times and remind them to be well mannered. As an adult, you are expected to participate in adult activities, but your responsibility as a parent doesn't end because someone else is watching your children.

Don't overreact if told your child is misbehaving, but respond. Referee an argument if it's between the children. Remove your child if the person complaining is an adult. It doesn't matter who's right or wrong. Chalk up disagreements between children to differences in the way they were raised, and find your child a new playmate.

You may have done an excellent job teaching proper behavior to your child. On reunion day, they may forget everything they've learned. Keep your child near you and maintain control as best you can. If children get too tired or over-excited, they can be a handful.

Your Contribution

The reunion is a short term event, lasting a few days at most. Look for common interests and enjoy the company of your family. Be tolerant of those who just can't seem to become part of the group. Give them an extra minute or two of your time when you see them. You won't be able to make them happy but you will feel good about yourself for trying.

No issue coming up in the course of the reunion is worth fighting about. Find your sense of humor and walk away from difficult situations in order to maintain peace. Your goal should be to have relatives think you're fun to know and that you enjoy being part of the family.

8

ACCOMMODATIONS

*O*nce your guest list has been confirmed, it's time to decide how to accommodate out-of-town relations. As the planner, envision the reunion as a part of your relative's vacation. Do your best to help locate lodgings that are convenient for both the reunion and the enjoyment of other activities in the area.

HOTELS AND MOTELS

When notifying out-of-town relatives of the reunion, include information regarding the availability and cost of rooms in the area. This can be gathered in a variety of ways. Contact the local Chamber of Commerce and ask for a listing of motels and hotels that are current Chamber members.

Or, take advantage of tour books put out by auto insurance companies such as Auto Club of America (AAA) and Allstate. These guidebooks list local hotels and motels giving the location, a brief description of the facilities, and room rates. Not every hotel or motel in the area is listed; only those facilities inspected and rated by the tour book staff are included. In addition to being a hotel and motel directory, these tour books list and rate local restaurants. Out-of-town guests will appreciate this information since they're unfamiliar with the area.

You can also gather information on accommodations by calling the local hotels and motels that are listed in the telephone book.

Check on group discounts (most hotels and motels will give you a discounted rate for your group), weekend specials, or rates that include tickets to tourist attractions at the same time you're inquiring on the availability and cost of the room. In most cases, there is a certain time in which reservations have to be made in order to take advantage of the group discount. This information should be provided with the accommodation list. It's also a nice touch to leave a basket of fruit and the family reunion schedule waiting in each hotel room. It'll start the family reunion on a high note by making out-of town relatives feel welcome.

Once a list has been compiled, make photocopies as needed and include them with the invitations. It's only necessary to send these lists to non-local relatives. Any extra weight to the invitation packet means additional postage.

CAMPGROUNDS

As a consideration for the wide variety of choices in accommodations, include information for those traveling in recreational vehicles or tent camping. Include the location of campgrounds, nightly rate, recreational vehicle hookup information, and the availability of showers and bathrooms.

A WIDE PRICE RANGE

It's a big mistake to make assumptions regarding other people. One family may be attending the reunion on a shoestring budget, while another may stay where twenty-four hour room service is available. Double check your list of hotels and motels to verify it includes every budget and lifestyle.

SEASONAL RATES

If the family reunion is scheduled to coincide with a holiday or a sporting event, you may have a problem getting accommodations. The more of a demand for rooms, the less the hotels and motels are willing to negotiate a lower rate. During the peak of the season or special events, it's important to book the rooms as early as possible. Even if a discount can't be given, your relatives will be assured a place to sleep.

LOCAL RELATIVES AS HOSTS

An alternative to having out-of-town relatives stay at a hotel, motel, or campground is to invite them to stay with local relatives who have extra room. The planning committee should make a list of the people who are willing to have relatives stay with them. Locate anyone with spare bedrooms, cots, or floor space. You may need them all before the reunion is over.

HOSTING CHILDREN

Ask those who are willing to host relatives their feelings regarding children. Unless they have children, they'll need to childproof their home and gather material to entertain their young house guests. Adults prefer privacy, but the kids can sleep in sleeping bags on the floor. Children won't mind if they're having a good time. Though elderly relatives may want house guests, there's the possibility they'd be better off without the commotion children bring. Not everyone is suited to having children as house guests.

PERSONAL NEEDS

Elderly house guests or those with disabilities may have special needs requiring extra care. Inquire on these needs before inviting them into a home. Special considerations include their ability to climb stairs, their use of equipment such as a wheelchair or walker, and dietary restrictions. Certain floor plans are inappropriate for some relatives. Remember, house guests need to be comfortable in order to enjoy the visit.

THE HOUSEHOLD SCHEDULE

During the initial chat with your house guests, let them know when you get up and when you go to bed. This tells them about the schedule they'll be a part of for the next few days. They'll want to know when the bathrooms are in use and when they should stay out of your way. Here's how to phrase your schedule:

> "We're glad you'll be spending the next few days here. Doug gets up for work at 5:00 A.M., and I leave the house at 7:15 A.M. After that, you'll have the place to yourselves until we get home at 4:30 P.M. By the way, we go to bed around ten."

PLANNING MEALS

It's up to the host family to determine how they want to handle eating arrangements. As soon as your house guests arrive, explain how you intend to handle meals. If you're on a tight budget and only able to provide sleeping space, make sure that is clear. Here are a few suggestions for working out meals:

- Let the house guests know you've cleaned off a shelf in the refrigerator for their food if they plan to cook and eat at home. Give directions to the local market.
- Provide an assortment of menus from local restaurants. Include both dine-in and take-out selections.
- Offer to go out and eat with them, but make it clear that it's "Dutch Treat!"
- Arrange to *swap* cooking the meals. You'll shop for, prepare, and clean up the meal one night and they'll do the same the next. Use old family favorites as the dinner theme both nights.

Whatever you decide, be clear on the arrangements. Most people are happy to go along with the program, they just need to know what's expected of them.

SPECIAL TOUCHES

Your guests know they are welcome because of your invitation to them, but here are a few easy-to-do touches to make their stay a little more special:

- Have their room spotlessly clean. This lets them know you were looking forward to their visit.

- Make available a selection of magazines, Since you may be unsure of their tastes, choose a variety. Borrow back issues from friends so it's not an expense.
- Supply a good reading light above the bed.
- Place a radio and an alarm clock in the bedroom.
- Put fresh flowers next to the bed. Even a single bloom in a bud vase will do.
- Have plenty of blankets available. Air them outside the day prior to their arrival.
- Set out clean towels and washcloths. Leave the towels in the bedroom so houseguests know they're for them. Keep a laundry hamper in the bedroom so guests know where to put dirty linen.
- Make a little bathroom treat basket for house guests. Buy sample size bubble bath, powder, Q-tips, soap, hair spray, and toothpaste. As a finishing touch to the basket, include a wine glass and a single serving bottle of wine.
- Keep a bowl of fruit on the kitchen table.
- Have crackers and cheese available for munching.
- Keep both the phone directory near the phone for quick reference.
- Make a spare key and put it on a key ring. Your guests can then come and go on their own schedule.

Wherever out-of-town guests decide to stay, set the groundwork for the accommodations and include this information with their reunion packet. They'll appreciate only having to make the decision on where to stay and not having to research the area. This may just be the deciding factor that convinces them to attend the reunion.

9

ACTIVITIES

A variety of activities for all ages makes for a successful reunion. You'll have scheduled activities (mealtime, guest of honor tributes), semi-scheduled events (competitive team events, children's games), and day-long events (conversation areas and photo album viewing). Plan enough activities to keep everyone busy, but resist the urge to over schedule. Also, be prepared to change the schedule to accommodate spontaneous activities.

THE FAMILY TREE

At the entrance of the reunion set up a poster of the basic family tree with space available on pre-cut leaves where relatives can list their ages, occupation, or hobbies.

This poster has two purposes. It gives people something to do when they arrive at the reunion. Some people need a few minutes to get their bearings when thrust into a crowd. The family chart provides an immediate distraction for them. It also provides a little background information on the relatives. Cousin Chris will feel more comfortable approaching his Great-uncle Jack and Aunt Kay knowing they share an interest in Chinese culture. The poster will promote the feeling of establishing or re-establishing relationships as well as meeting relatives.

SUMMER TIME CHOICES

Picnics in the park are a favorite for family reunions. Everyone knows exactly what to expect at these parties. The day will be spent playing baseball, basketball, volleyball, or swimming. There will be activities for children such as a wheelbarrow race, an egg or water balloon toss, a scavenger hunt, and a softball throwing contest. Many outdoor type games are also available such as jarts, frisbee, and horseshoe. Encourage guests to bring some of their favorite outdoor games.

Children are so active, it's impractical to think you'll be able to keep them still during the reunion. Make sure the chosen location has a playground area as well as open spaces for organized games. During the planning process, solicit volunteers to staff a play center for the little ones.

Try to have small prizes available for children who participate in the games. If you plan on limiting the prizes to one per child, announce this at the beginning of the game period. Unless prizes are limited, a few children who may be more athletic than the rest will get most of the prizes. Solicit volunteers to help with the expense of purchasing these prizes, or ask each relative to bring a WRAPPED prize suitable for the age group of their youngest child. Have them mark the outside of the package with the age and sex of the intended recipient. This way children of all age groups get prizes.

If family members are bringing prizes, suggest a price level so all participants receive a roughly equivalent prize. The prize should be a token gift, not an expensive item. You might suggest that the guests choose among the following when purchasing a gift for the reunion:

picture books	fast food gift certificates
puzzles	sidewalk chalk
kaleidoscopes	balls
beach and sand toys	coloring book and crayons
stuffed animals	play dough

Children enjoy participating in activities with grown-ups. Set aside time during the day for games such as egg toss, sack races, and tug-of-war where children and adults are on the same team. When it's time to choose partners, let the children do the picking. They'll quickly ask the adults to join in the fun!

Almost assuredly, at some point during the day, there will be a competitive team activity such as baseball, volleyball, or basketball, between adults and their teenage (or older) children. The winning generation will have bragging rights until the next reunion, as well as material with which to tease the losers throughout the year.

Organize bingo, horseshoe, cribbage, and card game areas for the adults. These games should be set up in shaded, non-windy areas of the picnic site. There should also be designated areas where people can sit and visit with each other. Take advantage of picnic tables, benches, and blankets on the ground. If needed, ask your relatives to bring their folding or lawn chairs for additional seating.

WINTER TIME CHOICES

Double check for dangerous situations before relatives arrive. Make sure the walkways and driveways are dry and clear of snow. There shouldn't be soft spots in the ice, nor obstacles in the toboggan run. Take a final walk through the reunion area specifically looking for trouble. It's best to find and correct a potential problem before the relatives arrive.

Don't limit the choices in recreation to team competitions. While football and hockey are expected activities, remember that some people are loners or prefer individual activities such as cross-country skiing or snowmobile riding. Other winter activities include sledding and tobogganing. Have plenty of sleds, or cardboard boxes available for people to join in the fun. The outdoor highlight of a winter reunion could be a cooperative snowman building project.

Some relatives may want to attend the reunion, but need or plan to spend most of their time indoors. You'll need a heated building where these people can stay. Entertain them with board and card games and set up plenty of chairs for conversational groups. This is a good place to show photo albums and old pictures and a good time to play the family video taken at the last reunion. Use background music to enhance the coziness of the room.

Children need to come in from the outdoors often. If they forget to come in on their own, parents should go after them. Children get caught up in the excitement of activities, so monitor their time outdoors carefully.

As they come in from outdoors, have plenty of blankets available for family members . Everyone likes cuddling up to get warm. Keep pots of coffee, tea, and hot chocolate brewing the whole day. If at all possible, try to have a clothes dryer on the site of a winter reunion. Those relatives who forgot a change of clothing to replace wet articles will appreciate the convenience.

DAY FUN

A daytime reunion includes all age groups, so activities should be planned to appeal to a broad audience. Young children are less able to entertain themselves, so the planner must insure there is always something for them to do. It's important to keep the children occupied, but still allow for adult interaction and conversation.

Whatever recreation is being planned, the attire of a daytime reunion should be casual. Make a point of reminding those with children to bring an extra change of clothing in case their child gets wet or dirty.

Finally, a daytime reunion has an ending point. When it gets dark, those who wish to continue the party are free to move it elsewhere, but the planned reunion activities have come to an end.

EVENING FUN

Evening reunions, by their nature, have a different type of dress and behavior. Children are less likely to be included since many of the activities will be taking place after their bedtime. If children are excluded from the reunion, make that very clear when sending out the invitations. A lone over-tired child, can easily put a damper on an adult gathering.

An evening reunion will generally be more costly to the participants since it involves more formal clothing and usually a sit-down dinner. Games and casual activities will be replaced by speeches, dancing, and conversation groups. At a formal evening reunion, you are likely to get to know a little less about your relatives. Everyone will be showing their more sedate side as a result of the formal atmosphere.

MEALTIME

The meal should be the focal point of the day. Stop all other activities and insist everyone eat at the same time, in the same area. The seating should encourage conversations as well as eating. Expect, however, there to be some stragglers and non-conformists. It's their reunion, too, so have a little flexibility. Invite relatives to identify the food they've brought and describe the recipe. Some old family recipes are sure to turn up on the dinner table. Encourage everyone to bring a copy of the recipe for the dish they passed. Keep the recipes together in a special box so they can be copied and sent to all attendees.

If there is a guest of honor, the tribute and gifts should take place after the meal. If there is no honored relative, the reunion coordinator can use the time after the meal to discuss the next reunion.

PROFESSIONAL PLANNERS

Professional party planners have more experience than the average person on how to entertain crowds. Their knowledge regarding what activity has and hasn't succeeded in the past could save much aggravation when planning your reunion. If you choose the professional planner route, the job of the reunion committee will be to give background on the family and offer suggestions on the direction they'd like to see the party take. From there, the professional planner will bring all the equipment and supplies, as well as a staff of workers on reunion day. Their presence will free everyone to fully enjoy themselves the day of the party.

If you consider hiring a professional planner, have them sign a contract describing exactly what they're responsible for. The contract must also spell out who is liable if things fail to go as planned or if an accident should occur.

A CRUISE

If the reunion will take place aboard a cruise ship, arrange with your travel agent to have special events scheduled once you're on board.

Depending on the size of your party, you may be able to negotiate for separate cocktail parties, a private dining room, and the use of conference rooms during the course of the excursion.

A cruise reunion will be costly, but there are a few ways to hold down the expenses. First, know approximately how many family members will be attending. A reunion will usually have enough people to fall under the group rate category. Secondly, many cabins on the ship accommodate more than two people and there's a special, lower rate for the third and fourth person in the room. For parents traveling with older children, there are connecting cabins. Parents can be close, but still have privacy.

When figuring the cost of a cruise reunion, remember that meals and shipboard entertainment (except casino bets and tips) are included in the price. A cruise can be a real bargain if scheduled when rates are lowest.

Hotel, Motel, or Resort

If you plan the reunion at a hotel or motel, there are already many activities incorporated into the setting. Game areas, swimming pools, restaurants, nightclubs, and rooms you can escape to are all in the same place. Hotels and motels have a staff on hand to do the cooking and cleaning, and may even have a list of baby-sitters. This type of facility works well for casual daytime activities followed by a more formal sit-down dinner in the evening. Some hotels and motels have an events coordinator on site to assist in your reunion plans. Utilize this person if they are available.

Family Entertainment

Regardless of the size of your family, if you ask, you'll find some amazing talents. Consider having a sign-up sheet posted so those with talents can show them off. Limit the time participants have in the limelight so everyone gets a chance to perform.

ENTERTAINMENT LOG

NAME	AGE	TALENT
Marshall	*10*	*Clarinet*

All family members who wish to participate in the talent show should sign up the day of the reunion. After family members have signed up to show off their talents, arrange a schedule of events.

ENTERTAINMENT SCHEDULE

12:15 A.M.   *Marcus and Alex singing*

Be on the lookout for skills that can be taught as well as shown. Take advantage of the fact that Uncle Rick used to play on a minor league baseball team. The kids will be impressed, even if it happened twenty years ago. Having Uncle Rick spend a half hour or so hitting balls and instructing how to throw properly can be a great experience for everyone. You may have a tennis pro, basketball hero, diving star, or skating champion in the family. Include every age in the instructions. Have everyone who is physically fit get up and participate. It's never too late to try new things.

Not all talents are sports related. If Aunt Cheryl spends a day each week as a storyteller at the preschool, she's the perfect candidate to entertain the children before nap time. Seek out unusual talents and showcase them.

THE TALENT LIST

When searching out talents within your family, look for some of the following:

Baseball, football, golf, or tennis player	Dance instructor
	Singer
Clown	Storyteller
Magician	Photographer
Mine	Musician
Wood carver	Face painter

Keeping the day or evening filled with plenty of activities will make the reunion a pleasant experience for all family members. Enjoy each other's special talents as you renew old friendships and begin new ones.

10

GUEST OF HONOR

*Y*ou may want to single out a person, couple, or group of family members at every reunion to be the guest(s) of honor. They will become the focal point of all attention and tributes. This is a nice tradition, giving both the guest of honor and the reunion participants a chance to make the day just a little more special.

CHOOSING THE GUEST OF HONOR

It is always appropriate to have a guest of honor at a family reunion and the most likely candidate is the family matriarch or patriarch. The reunion will become their *day* with special times or activities planned around them. This works especially well if the reunion is scheduled to coincide with a birthday or anniversary.

Instead of honoring a single guest, you may want to choose multiple guests of honor. For example, you can single out your mother and all her siblings, or all family members of a certain age, or all people whose birthday falls within a month either way of the reunion date. This is ideal for a first reunion, especially if it is uncertain as to whether there is going to be a second. Grouping family members is also appropriate if the reunions occur so often that you're running out of family members to honor. Here again, you need to be creative. Some potential guests of honor are recent college graduates or anyone who just received their drivers licenses.

For multiple guests of honor, permit each to introduce themselves and their family unit. Since the families will vary in size, set a time limit for each speaker. Speakers can use this time to update all guests on news and events since the last visit. Have speakers cover relevant topics such as weddings, births, deaths, graduations, and engagements. If someone is doing well in their job or starting their own business, now is the time to mention it. A long winded speaker may bore the crowd so set and stick with time limits for each person.

NOTIFYING THE GUEST OF HONOR

Once a potential guest of honor is identified, call up and ask:

"Grandma Ann, as you know, we're planning the reunion this year for the Fourth of July weekend and we'd like you to be our guest of honor. You've had some great experiences so we feel you'd be the perfect choice to be our special guest."

After the guest of honor has accepted, ask him or her:

"Is there anything special we can include in the reunion to make your day more meaningful?"

Try to fill any and all requests!

Mention the guest of honor in the invitation. In addition to the organized tributes, allow and encourage family members to come up with surprises of their own. That way, the guest of honor will have a variety of attention throughout the day.

REMINISCING TIME

Allow the guest of honor enough time to reminisce and speak of family memories. The best time for speeches is after the meal. Prior to the guest of honor making their speech, show home movies, videos, slides, or any other type of audio-visual presentation of their life. A pleasant surprise is to play pre-recorded tributes from family members who were unable to attend.

After the guest of honor has spoken, family members can provide brief commentary on their special memories of that person. Include all age groups and relationships so every aspect of their life is covered. This can be done in a serious manner or as a *roast* style, but get permission from the guest of honor before proceeding.

A photo poster is a simple, inexpensive tribute. Ask the guests to bring a photograph that evokes a special moment or memory involving the guest of honor. Make sure the photo has information regarding the date and occasion shown, as well as the name of the person bringing the photo. Arrange these pictures on poster board as the guests arrive. Display the photographs by year, family unit, or activity involved (such as parties, vacations, or private moments). After the reunion, the planning committee is responsible for getting this poster framed. Make sure those bringing photos aren't expecting them to be returned to avoid any misunderstandings at the end of the day.

Commission the most artistic member of the family to draw a representation of the family tree. The artwork can be as simple or elaborate as you choose, just make sure it's large and framed. Your gift will be most appreciated if it can go directly from the party to the wall with no extra effort by the recipient.

The family tree should be presented by the closest relative to the guest of honor. If it's to be presented to a parent, all children should be on stage to do the presenting. If it's for a brother or sister, all other siblings should be present. Include everyone.

THOUGHTFUL TRIBUTES

Recognition can come in many forms. From a card signed by all relatives attending to a proclamation by the local mayor, tributes will brighten the guest of honor's day. Here are more suggestions:

- Give them a corsage or boutonniere
- Have children decorate their chair as a throne
- Write a poem in their honor
- Present them with a plaque
- Act out a short play about an event in their life
- Make a donation in their name to a favorite charity

FOR THOSE NOT PRESENT

Always take a brief moment at family reunions to remember family members who have passed away since the last gathering. This should be done by either the next of kin or the master of ceremonies. A few moments of remembering the happy times will be appreciated by everyone. Use a brief sentence such as:

> "Grammy Stuligross died last December, but she often commented that her happiest moments were spent being with her children and grandchildren."

A simple statement like the one above is an excellent way of connecting the past and present.

CELEBRATING BABIES

Babies symbolize family continuity. Let the proud moms and dads have their moment to brag and show off. This can be done as part of the official agenda or incorporated throughout the day. A poster board can be set up to hold baby photos or birth announcements. If parents or grandparents want to show off additional pictures, they'll probably gather in this area of the room with their brag books.

If parents are permitted to introduce new arrivals, set a cutoff age (under one year), as well as a time limit for them to speak of their child.

INTRODUCING SPOUSES

The newlywed spouse may be the most uncomfortable person at a reunion. Since the new husband or wife may know very few people, their spouse will want to show them off to everyone. Set aside a table that is decorated in wedding motif so all newlyweds can display their photo albums. At a dinner, all newlyweds could rise for a toast or the first dance of the evening could be dedicated to them.

HONOR THE REUNION PLANNERS

The people who spent a lot of time or money organizing the reunion should be publicly recognized for this effort. If you're the sole organizer, you can't get up and pat yourself on the back, but you can (and should) recruit someone to do it for you.

During your moment of recognition, discuss why you thought a reunion was a good idea, what you hoped to accomplish with the party, and which of your goals you achieved. This is a good time to account, with humor, some of the obstacles you encountered. This is not the time to speak in a negative manner about anyone—regardless of the trouble they gave you.

The reunion planner should be the last person to speak. If a committee was involved, the chairperson should present each member a memento for their planning efforts. An engraved photo frame would be an appropriate gift. Upon completion of the speeches, the chairperson should begin discussing the date, location, and chairperson of the next reunion. If all went as planned, you'll have people standing in line to plan the next one!

11

THEMES

*L*et your imagination run wild and be at your creative best when deciding on the theme for your family reunion. This is probably the most enjoyable part of the planning process because the *fun* in you is able to come out. Tie the invitations, attire, food selections, and game prizes to the theme. You can tease your family members by telling them little details of the reunion day plans and informing them they'll have the opportunity to step away from everyday life and into the excitement of meeting with their relatives. By making sure your theme is appropriate to all ages attending the party, you encourage full participation by everyone.

WESTERN BARBECUE

There are picnics and then there are western style picnics. Going western means you'll find activities that both young and not-so-young family members will enjoy. This is a good theme to use if you're planning to meet at a traditional park setting.

Begin the western theme by designing boot shaped, paper invitations stating:

Front: Dig out your denims, boots, and hats for the 15th Annual Oliver Reunion.

Inside: Pack up the family and head on down to the reunion on the first Sunday in May (the 4th) beginning at 10:00 A.M. Bring your own main course to grill and a side dish (feeding eight) to share. Meet at Flat Rock Park to enjoy some family fun. Grandma Buleah, the guest of honor, will be on hand to tell stories of our family. We're planning games for the cowboys and cowgirls, so let us know the ages of your children. Send back the enclosed postcard by April 1st so we know who'll be attending.

Back: Use this space to give directions to the reunion site.

On the reunion day, borrow a boom box (large portable radio) from a teenager and play country western music as the family approaches the picnic site. Lively music will give the feeling of *western* and get your relatives in the proper frame of mind for the day.

At the check-in area, pass out name tags in the shape of sheriff badges. Color code the badges for each branch so you can identify who belongs together. If you're purchasing souvenirs, straw cowboy hats, with the reunion name and date imprinted on a removable bandanna, is the perfect choice.

After the relatives have checked in, direct them to the family tree diagram, which has been designed in the western theme with cowboy boots, branding irons, and ten gallon hats to update their information. When you look back at these boards in future years, you'll be able to tell your theme at a glance.

Dress the master of ceremonies in a western outfit. Whenever this person speaks, instruct him or her to refer to the good old days on the ranch, sitting around the family homestead and other western terminology.

Others at the reunion can have a chance to dress in a western outfit, too. Hire a photographer specializing in old-fashioned dress portraits to come take pictures for a few hours. Each family can take turns donning western garb and having a family portrait taken.

Keep up the western theme with your guest of honor gift. You may want to present this person with a silver belt buckle with the reunion information engraved, a hand tooled leather belt with their name, or a broad-brimmed high-crowned felt hat.

Consider hiring someone to teach an hour of square or line dancing if no one in your family has that talent. All ages can participate in this activity, and it's fun. Limit most scheduled activities to an hour. It's better if family members are begging for more time and activity than questioning if it'll ever end!

To keep everything centered around the western theme, the prizes for the children should include such items as cowboy belts, fringed vests, leather pouches, and authentic cowgirl jump ropes. Recruit a family member to *brand* the children as they arrive at the reunion. This can be done by writing the family name on their arm with a magic marker (make sure it's the kind that washes off). They'll think it's neat to be branded.

End the day sitting around a campfire strumming guitars and singing songs. Include the standard western songs and family favorites. This is a nice wind-down activity to calm children for the drive home.

This theme is relaxed, friendly, and very suited to an out-of-doors reunion. It's the kind of theme where your family would be surprised if you didn't say in your best western drawl, "Y'all come back next year, ya hear."

LUAU

This theme is a great way to utilize an ocean, lake, or swimming pool. You can take advantage of planning activities around the setting without bringing in a lot of props for your activities. Kids will be especially interested in going where they can play in water.

For the invitation, find the brightest paper available and use stamp pads or stickers to make a colorful flower border. Spray the invitation with floral scented cologne to involve the sense of smell as well as the eyes when first receiving the invitation. An 8 1/2 x 11-inch invitation could read:

WHAT:	A Day in the Tropics
WHO:	Kull Family
WHERE:	Metropolitan Beach (directions on back)
TIME:	Any time after 11:00 A.M.
WHY:	Celebrate the 10th anniversary of Sue and Dave
ATTIRE:	Flowered shirts, grass skirts, shorts, leis, bathing suits
BRING:	An appetizer for a dozen people
	Towels
	Any photos of Sue and Dave (photos won't be returned)
	A ukulele or guitar
R.S.V.P.	Call Idell at 555-1234 between 5:00 P.M. and 7:00 P.M. any week day prior to July 1st and let her know whether or not you'll be attending.

At the entrance of the reunion site play Hawaiian music. Surround the check-in area with potted palms and distribute flower shaped name tags (this is something children can help make in advance) with a different flower for each family branch. Make sure everyone gets a paper lei and a kiss on each cheek as they enter.

Decorate the tables in the same color as the invitations and load them up with as many fresh flowers as you can gather. If your site includes a pool, decorate the surrounding area to look lush and tropical. You can float fresh flowers in the swimming pool before or after people get into the swim of things.

Neon baseball caps or visors featuring the family name and reunion date solves the souvenir question. Call advertising specialties in the Yellow Pages. The prizes for children's games can include beach towels, sandbox toys, and sunglasses.

Create an arch of fresh or paper flowers to use around the seating area for your guest of honor. This is a visual way to separate the honoree from the rest of the group. Since you've requested family members to bring photos, display them on poster board. Present the guest of honor with a frame the size of the photo poster. This now makes a lovely gift that goes from the reunion to the home with no effort in between.

As a reminder, since you'll be planning activities both in and around the water, make sure there is constant supervision of the children. Consider hiring a certified lifeguard to help monitor the water. Family members, distracted by ongoing activities can forget to watch the children.

This theme takes advantage of the water as the main source of entertainment. On a hot summer day, the promise of keeping cool is a great way to entice the family to a gathering.

SOCK HOP

A 1950's sock hop theme can be used at both an indoor or outdoor reunion as well as a day or evening affair. Carry out the theme throughout the day with music and activities, and include a costume contest.

Invitations can be simple, but fun. Fold an 8 1/2 x 11-inch, invitation weight paper in half or cut and fold to fit your envelope. You'll find interesting papers at paper supply stores, or try your stationers. While you're at it, buy the envelopes, too.

On the front side of the folded paper, print a list of the all-time, top 10 rock "n" roll tunes. Call your local radio station or music store for help. Dot the white space around the list with half and quarter notes. On the inside, print the party invitation. You can print this yourself or take the paper and information to an instant printer and have them do the printing and folding.

WHY:	Rock "n" Rollin' Good Time
	5th Annual Sydell Family Reunion
WHEN:	February 19th—the fiftieth day of the year
WHERE:	Dana Point Hilton, Pacific Coast Highway Exit
	Dana Point, California
	(714) 555-1253
	(when calling for reservations ask for the Sydell family reunion discount and request rooms on the 3rd floor)
TIME:	Rooms are available at noon on Friday, and the reunion will begin Saturday after breakfast with children's games in the pool at 9:00 A.M.
BRING:	Bathing suits (there is an indoor pool and jacuzzi)
	Your favorite record from the fifties
	Any pictures of yourself taken during the fifties
MEALS:	A buffet lunch will be served at noon and a sit down dinner will begin at 6:00 P.M. Make checks for food payable directly to the hotel. Lunch is $6.00 per adult and $4.00 per child.
	Dinner prices are $13.00 and $6.00 respectively.
	Chicken, fish, and beef will be available for dinner.
FUN:	Use of all hotel facilities during the day
	(A schedule of all reunion events will be posted by the third floor elevator)
	Awards for best male, female, and child costume presented after dinner
	Sock hop begins at 8:00 P.M. (phone numbers for sitters are available at the hotel desk)
RSVP	Contact the hotel directly for accommodations
	Call Carol or Gertrude at (213) 555-2734 and let us know whether or not you'll be joining the group.

Schedule pool games for children as the first activity at the hotel. It will get them off to an active start and give the adults a chance to get together.

Put a ball or other object at the bottom of the pool for swimmers to find, organize speed competitions, form teams for relay races, conduct best mermaid and merman contests, and determine the biggest splash. Towels, pool toys, and tokens for the video games in the lobby arcade are good prizes for these events.

Check into using a conference room during the reunion. It will be useful for a bingo game or the family talent show. Both of these events need to take place in the afternoon since the evening will be taken up with the sock hop. In addition to a full schedule of activities, leave time for napping and being alone.

Following the meal, pour beverages into souvenir coffee mugs displaying the reunion name and date. Advertising specialties in the Yellow Pages can help find the mugs. Give mugs to every adult, whether or not they drink coffee.

After the tables have been cleared, it's time to show off the costumes and award prizes for the most authentic. Ask the disc jockey or master of ceremonies to play appropriate music while the judging is taking place. Grab your camera because this will be a great photo opportunity. You'll want to save the pictures for the next family reunion. Prizes can include compact discs of fifty's music, a piece of antique jewelry, or a fifty's leather jacket. At the end of the contest, invite everyone to dance.

This type of reunion is perfect for allowing lots of time for family interaction. On reunion day, since there is no cooking or cleaning up to be done, family members can focus on visiting and socializing.

BLACK AND WHITE SEMI-FORMAL

The most romantic evening you can imagine can be planned using this theme. This will be an adult only function held at an elegant restaurant. Those family members who enjoy party dress will be looking forward to this event.

Enlist the help of a family member that can either do calligraphy or has beautiful penmanship. Purchase blank white or cream invitations. Use black ink to print an eye-catching summons to your relatives. The printed invitation should follow the etiquette rules that are in keeping with the semi-formal theme.

Front: **CELEBRATE OUR FAMILY**

Inside: Guerami Family Reunion
Saturday, July 15
Stardust Room, Hyatt Regency—Santa Ana

5:00 P.M.	cocktails and check-in
6:00 P.M.	dinner
7:00 P.M.	family updates
8:00 P.M.	dancing

Cost: $35 per person, payable at check-in
R.S.V.P.: Charlene and Jim (714) 555-2345
Attire: Black and white semi-formal

Back: Use this space for written directions to the hotel, as well as a map. Include the hotel phone number in case people get lost on the way.

As a final touch to the invitations include sparkly confetti in the envelope. Don't put in so much that a mess is made when the invitation is opened— just enough to simulate stardust!

Set up your check-in area outside the ballroom door. Collect the meal money but don't issue name tags. Since everyone is in semi-formal attire, there isn't a convenient way to attach the name tag without the risk of snagging or leaving an adhesive on the clothing. Instead, set out formal name card on the table identifying each relative and the family branch they represent.

Inform the hotel meeting planner you are having a black and white theme so the tables are set with cloths and dishes accordingly. Red is a good accent color to use at this event. You may want to have single red flowers in bud vases. At the end of the party encourage the guests to take the flowers.

An arch of black and white helium balloons as you enter the ballroom will immediately set the mood for the evening. Keep the room well lit in the early portion of the reunion to encourage mingling. Later, have softer lighting and a glitter ball for a more romantic atmosphere.

After the meal, spend time catching up on each others lives. Reserve enough microphone time for the head of each family to give their update. If there is additional time before the band or disk jockey arrives, ask the oldest family members to tell stories of their youth. They will enjoy reminiscing and everyone present will learn a little more about the family.

Pre-arrange special dances to celebrate people and events. These can include a dance for those married a year or less, married 25 or 50 years, with grandchildren, a complete branch of the family, a generation, and those who came from out of town.

Arrange for a photographer to take individual and group pictures. Or, have one or two members of the group circulate with an instant photo camera. Slip the pictures in holders with the reunion name and date. Remind everyone to take their flower as they depart.

This theme gives the adults a wonderful opportunity to take a break from children and work responsibilities and enjoy being a grown-up with an extended family.

ZOO SAFARI

Planning your reunion in a setting such as the local zoo gives you a built-in theme. All zoos have public grounds where you can set up your picnic and relaxation area.

Encourage the family to start thinking about the reunion activity by playing a game that matches animals to their babies. Put two columns of names, side by side, on the front of the invitation. The animal's name is in one column and the baby's name is in the second column. Ask the reader to match the names. For example, what animal would you match to the name joey? Try for a mix of easy and hard pairs. Your library or zoo will be a good source of information if you get stuck. At the bottom of the invitation, announce there will be a prize at the reunion for the most right answers. Write the party information on the inside of the invitation.

WHAT:	Flores Family Fun Reunion
WHERE:	Montabello Zoo
	(picnic section off parking lot A)
WHEN:	First Saturday in May (May 2)
BRING:	Main course for your family plus a vegetable dish to share (for 12)
	Camera
	Comfortable shoes
RSVP:	Call the answering machine of Irene and Rudy (781-521-8593) by April 1. Before giving your message, please do your favorite animal imitation. Prizes will be awarded at the reunion for best animal imitations!

Check with the administrative office at the zoo to arrange both regular tours and behind the scene tours for your family. Most zoos have special programs in place for groups. If your reunion is large, try to arrange different tours for the children based on their ages. Younger kids have less of an attention span than those who are older.

Find out when the animals are fed. Children and adults will enjoy watching mealtime in the lion den or at the penguin house.

After lunch, slip your answering machine tape into a cassette recorder and play back the best animal imitations called in. Give T-shirts depicting the imitated animal to the proud winners. Give a wind sock imprinted with the zoo's logo for the match the animals game winner.

Games for the children can be the next order of business. Since there is probably less space available at a zoo than in a park, your games may include a spelling bee of animal names, drawing and coloring of the best zebra, bird calls, and guessing the height of the giraffe. Animal books or animal noses make good prizes for these activities.

Even though space may be limited, plan to showcase the family talent. This can work if there is a place the audience can sit quietly and not disturb other zoo visitors. Family members can display dancing, magic tricks, singing, and joke telling at this time. Offer animal crackers as snacks during the program.

T-shirts with the reunion name, date, and theme would be a welcome gift in this informal setting such as the zoo. Select the same bright color for every shirt, but a different animal for each family branch. These shirts will be appreciated if one of your family members wanders away from the group and needs to be spotted in a crowd.

A day at the zoo is traditionally a family activity. Incorporating it with a reunion gives adults and children the advantage of time together with their immediate and extended family. This theme is an example of fully utilizing the setting.

For those who haven't guessed . . . a joey is a baby kangaroo.

FAMILY HERITAGE FEAST

Whatever your heritage, celebrate it during the reunion. This is a great time to pull out all the stops and get as close as possible to duplicating the spirit of past generations..

Choose an appropriate ethnic restaurant or, lacking that, decorate a private room in a restaurant or hall. Hang banners with the family crest around the room. If you don't have a family crest, make one up or borrow one. Include national dishes in the menu. Serve desserts such as English bread and butter pudding, summer pudding, trifle, or plum pudding; Austrian/German strudel, linzer torte, sacher torte, or black forest cake; or French profiterole, flan, roulade, or crepe suzette.

The invitations should have the family crest on the outside and the necessary information should be in the center section. It would be a nice touch to enclose a symbol of your heritage such as a drawing of a four leaf clover, edelweiss, fleur de lis, or lotus in the invitation.

Front	Holmdahl Family Members
	Hear Ye! Hear Ye!
	Come One, Come All
Inside:	10th Annual Reunion
	HaufHouse Restaurant
	Saturday, October 12
	1:00 P.M. until 6:00 P.M.
	Guest of Honor—Aunt Brigitte turns 40 this year
	Send check for $15.00 to cover bratwurst lunch in the enclosed, stamped envelope. There will be a no-host bar for those who wish to purchase alcoholic beverages.
Back:	Use this space for the address and map to the restaurant and the restaurant's phone number.

Remember to enclose a stamped, self-addressed envelope to make it easy for family members to reply.

A restaurant/bar of this sort would know an authentic band for hire. Encourage everyone to get up and dance, especially when it's ethnic dance time.

This theme incorporates fun with heritage tradition. Family reunions encourage pride in your heritage, so go back to your original roots for inspiration when planning this party.

CARNIVAL TIME

This is every child's favorite. Here kids are allowed to be the bouncy happy creatures they were meant to be. Every moment of the day is set up to be appreciated by someone between the ages of two and ten. The atmosphere here is kid paradise.

For the invitation, cut a clowns head with a pointy hat from bright construction paper. Use a contrasting colored crayon to write the invitation, directing it to the children.

Outside:	Calling all children in the Hellyar family—grab your parents, aunts, uncles, and grandparents and come to the 16th reunion.
Inside:	Meet at Uncle Mike and Aunt Danielle's house on June 1st at 11:00 A.M. Bring your throwing arm to play catch, legs for races, eyes for searching for pennies in the sand, and lots of smiles. Ask your parents to bring a cake along with them. Call us at (704)555-8079 to let us know if you're coming.

On the day of the reunion, play carnival music over a loud speaker so it can be heard as the children arrive at your house. You want the children to almost go into excitement overload before they reach the front door. In the yard, set up various games of skill such as ball toss, a basketball hoop, and penny pitching. Have a large supply of inexpensive trinkets to hand out for winning a game. Shop at a party supply store where you can get large bags of rings, miniature cars, head bands, and drinking straws. These are the kinds of prizes kids love to win.

In addition to the children's prizes, set up a photo taking booth with the family name and reunion date. Take instant photos of individuals and groups and immediately turn these photos into buttons to wear. Check party supply stores and camera shops for button making equipment. The buttons can be saved as a memento of the reunion and are fun to wear during the day.

Children like hot dogs but if you really want to impress them, rent snow cone and cotton candy machines. Don't forget the popcorn. Now this is the kind of stuff that will have them begging their parents to bring them to the next reunion!

Design a miniature golf course that runs from the front yard, through the side yard, and into the backyard. Use frisbees instead of golf balls, with tires, wading pools, laundry baskets, and other receptacles as targets. Play individually or as teams. Have some toys on hand such as hula hoops, baseball gloves, old maid card games, or bubbles to blow for the children's amusement. You may also want a supply of nintendo games in case of bad weather.

Before it's time to go home, enlist a few family members to do face painting. Give children simple choices such as hearts, stars, or spiders. Face painting forces the children to sit still so it has the effect of calming them for the ride home. Make this the last activity of the day so they don't get wound up again.

Children love attention and love to play. While they are enjoying themselves, the adults have time to catch up on family news. This is an especially appropriate reunion when there are lots of young children in the family.

12

THEME STARTERS

*I*t only takes one or two good ideas to add pizazz to your family reunion. Take these bits and pieces of themes and see where they'll take you. Once you find an idea you like, you can easily apply it to your party.

TRAVEL TREASURES

Whether you've traveled to exotic locations or vacationed close to home, everyone has a memory to share. There's always the perfect photo to view and the story to tell of the fish that got away. Plan a reunion specifically designed to share all the ups and downs of the celebrated *family vacation.*

This theme can be used for any casual dress, private home reunion. Proper attire might be a T-shirt depicting a place you've visited or a landmark you enjoyed seeing. Everyone should be encouraged to bring photos of their favorite trip.

For the invitations, go to a stationery store and look for paper with a world map background. If this is unavailable, any paper that suggests exotic, far-away places will do. Now, let your relatives know the activities of the reunion. Ask them to bring a dish to share that is reminiscent of the place they visited, photos of the trip, and an edited (five minute maximum length) video of their adventure.

Decorate the house with travel posters (borrow them from your travel agent), including a large one covering the front door. Hang them from the ceiling in addition to taping them to the walls. Set hotel soap out in the bathroom for atmosphere.

Once everyone has arrived, begin showing the videos. Each family can give a brief introduction to their video by telling why they chose that destination and how they felt about the trip. Give out travel related gifts such as folding umbrellas, plastic containers for toiletries, disposable panoramic cameras, or film developing gift certificates as prizes for best videos.

When sitting down to the meal, invite everyone to identify and describe the recipes for the exotic dishes they brought. If there is time, some of the relatives who traveled to far away places may want to describe mealtime rituals in those countries.

Give everyone a key ring imprinted with "Kelly Family Reunion" as they depart. It will be a daily reminder of the reunion.

SUPER BOWL WINNER

This is an ideal theme for a winter reunion held at the home of a family member. All the entertainment you need for this reunion is a television set and plenty of floor space. Invite the relatives to start arriving at least two hours before the big game so there is time for socializing. You may even want to play your own pre-Super Bowl scrimmage in the yard if time and space permit such an activity.

For the invitations, cut headlines out of the newspaper connected with football and the big game. Glue these to make a border around the edges of an 8 1/2 x 5 1/2-inch sheet of paper and write the reunion information in the middle. On the front lawn, put out huge signs naming the two competing teams. Invite your relatives to sign their names to the sign of the team they hope will win. Frame the doorway with pom poms and pennants featuring the colors of the competing teams. Use each team's color scheme with the napkins and paper plates so you can tell who is cheering for which team.

Organize a pool to see if anyone can guess the final score of the game. If more than one person chooses the same score, give them the option to change their pick or agree to share the winnings. A good gift for this reunion would be a mug with the reunion date and the names of the competing teams.

CHILI COOK-OFF

What better time than the Fourth of July to hold a chili cook-off family reunion. This theme takes advantage of friendly competition as the method of getting some really yummy food to the party. Encourage cook-off competition starting with the invitation continuing through the awarding of the grand prize.

Using a paper plate for the invitation, invite your relatives and challenge them at the same time. Invitations should read:

> I, Wayne Mitchell, extend this invitation to the 1st Annual Reunion and Chili Cook-off. Bring yourself, your family, and your favorite chili to Kodiak Park on the Fourth of July. Prizes will be given for best spicy, vegetarian, and overall chili. Let's meet at 2:00 P.M. with the judging at 3:00 P.M. The family will dine on our masterpieces after the judging.

> There will be a fireworks display visible from our picnic site beginning at 9:00 P.M. Bring blankets and jackets if you're planning to stay since it gets chilly in this area after dark.

Make sure your reunion site has plenty of stoves to heat the chili as it arrives. Give every person who brings a container of chili a chef's apron you've marked "1st Annual Reunion and Chili Cook-off Competitor". Use permanent markers in four different colors for the letters. Insist everyone wear their apron during the chili judging and while posing for group pictures.

HOUSE PROJECT

If you know an elderly relative who is in need of major home repairs or maintenance, you may want to schedule the yearly reunion at their place and tackle the fix-up project.

This is when a handwritten, letter style invitation is most appropriate. Find nice, basic stationery and write:

> Aunt Charlotte has been a real help to most of us in her lifetime, and now we'd like to repay her. This year, instead of the traditional picnic,

we're going to meet at her house which is located at _____ in _(the city of)_. She needs major work done (painting the garage, washing the walls, changing the shelf paper in the kitchen) as well as basic cleaning so bring your tools, paint brushes, and kind heart.

Aunt Charlotte only knows we'd like to use her house for the reunion this year so don't let it slip that the clean-up activities of the day are for her. Call John at _____ with regrets only. Please bring the children—there's enough to keep everyone busy.

A reunion of this sort is a wonderful tribute because it helps the guest of honor in a practical way. Also, it will accomplish in one day what would take many hours and dollars otherwise.

CELEBRATE THE OLDEST AND THE YOUNGEST

Reunions highlight continuous changes in the size and makeup of the family. One year you may choose to simultaneously honor both the oldest and youngest family members. Mention the oldest in the invitation (get their permission first—some members of the older generation may not want their ages known) and hint that there is a lot of competition for the youngest member. This is especially appropriate if there are numerous pregnant relatives.

Use a flyer type invitation for this reunion and set it up as a proclamation.

Come one, come all to the 17th Annual Taube reunion. Meet in the same place (Griffith Park), on the same day (the first Saturday in June—the 4th) beginning at 11:00 A.M. This year we will be celebrating our oldest and youngest members. Great-Aunt Rose Rebillot, who will be 94 this year promises to be on hand to collect the prize as the oldest member. It'll be interesting to meet our newest member since there are four relatives vying for this honor. Remember, you must attend to win the prize.

The gifts for the guests of honor could be a watch for the oldest symbolizing the passage of time, and a camera for the parents of the youngest symbolizing the recording of events to come.

Relay-Race Runs

Do you have fitness freaks in the family? Chances are some members dance, exercise, play tennis, or jog. Set up a relay team of these family members and run an agreed number of miles in an annual race. As waistlines and ages increase, so will the running times. When that happens, encourage the younger generation to join the competition and see who has the better times.

Invitations need to be issued to tie the cheering section in with the runners. Announce the time the race begins and where the cheering section will be located. Your invitations could read this way:

> Kathy, Warren, Arnold, Ernie, and Thomas will be racing in the Annual Phoenix Run. They could use our support. The race begins at 9:00 A.M. on Camelback Road. We encourage you to stand anywhere on the route to cheer them on, but plan to meet at the finish line by 11:30 A.M. for a big Simmons family cheer when they get to the end. We'll be returning to grandma's house for lunch beginning at 1:00 P.M.

> Bring any pictures or videos you have from last year's event and we'll review them before discussing this year's race. The runners have put a lot of time and energy into their training so be there to support the "Swift Simmons".

Anyone who competes in athletic events knows the importance of a cheering section. Planning a reunion around family participation in a sporting event is a great way of showing support and having fun.

Hollywood Stars

LIGHTS, CAMERA, ACTION!!!! Here's a reunion you can have lots of fun with. Decorate your reunion site to resemble a Hollywood premiere. From the time you greet your guests with a video microphone, to the time they leave in their personalized Hollywood *incognito* sunglasses (the party favor), everyone will feel they've attended a *celebrity opening.*

Design your invitations using lots of glitter and sparkle. This is the perfect time to put plenty of confetti in the envelope. And, make sure you're pouring champagne (alcoholic and non-alcoholic).

Most of us wish for a life more dramatic than we really live so put a little drama in your family. It'll be enjoyable to live in a fantasy world for a few hours.

For entertainment, give everyone a chance at the karaoke machine (an electronic sing-along machine). This will keep everyone occupied for a long time.

VINTAGE YEAR

Remember when? Pick out a year and tie the party to family events that occurred during the selected year. Choose a menu that represents that year. If the year isn't too far back, compliment the meal with a bottle(s) of wine from that vintage. Music of the time is something else that will place the family in the spirit of things. Bring pictures and memories which highlight the family events of that year including births, deaths, marriages, family moves, new pets, landmark birthdays, retirements, new home,s, new jobs, or winning the lottery.

At this type of reunion, allow every family member who can remember the year to contribute. It will be interesting to see how age, gender, and geographical differences affect the memories of your relatives.

Try to find a souvenir of the year to give as a gift. This may be a peace sign necklace, pet rock, or mood ring. Check out antique stores, flea markets, or garage sales to gather a large quantity of these items.

TIME CAPSULE

This is an interesting theme to use for a large family with a wide range of ages. The idea is to give each family a small container to fill with mementos that represents them as a group. Each family will create its own time capsule and then, at the reunion, all the small containers will be sealed together in a large waterproof container (possibly a large 33 gallon garbage can) to be opened at a future reunion in twenty years.

For the invitation, get an assortment of containers with tight fitting lids. These should include various sizes and shapes to make it interesting for your relatives to decide what to put inside. The postal service will deliver these containers as they are; just make sure they are properly addressed and have postage affixed.

Inside the container, place your invitation which should read:

Colker Family

Define yourselves through a time capsule. Join Jean, Maurice, and Bob at the Sarasota Park Recreation Center on September 16th beginning at noon for the 7th Semi-annual Colker Family Reunion. Bring your time capsule (or mail ahead if you're unable to attend) as they will be sealed in the *vault*, not to be reopened until the reunion twenty years from now. Fill this container with anything you feel symbolizes your family.

Bring a dish to pass as we reminisce about the past and make predictions about the future. DON'T FORGET TO FILL THIS CONTAINER FOR YOUR TIME CAPSULE CONTRIBUTION!

During the day, talk about memorable events in the family history. This is a good way of keeping children informed about family history. A final activity for a time capsule reunion would be to have family members predict what they will be doing in five or ten years. Questions could include where will I be working, what car will I be driving, how will I look, will I have children (grandchildren) and what hobby will I have. Get a volunteer to print out the responses and bring them to the future designated reunion.

OLD TYME KITCHEN PARTY

Anyone who remembers Grandma's pie will love this get-together. Everyone is invited to bring favorite family recipe dishes. Send invitations that depict an old-fashioned scene and use plain white and blue china at the party. Aim for a rural farmhouse look at the reunion site. Encourage family members to relate old stories or brand new ones as an *everyone participates* activity. Guests will go home with as many new old-family recipes as they care to jot down.

13

LET'S DO IT AGAIN

*Y*ou've just had a fun and successful day. It seems as though the family may want the reunion to be more than a one-time activity. This is the time to do some planning for the next event. You can either have the entire group participate in planning the next reunion, or invite those interested to form a sub-group.

A vote should be taken to determine whether the next reunion should be held in one year, five years, somewhere in between, or not at all. Since your relatives had a good time at this year's affair, it's likely they'll be looking forward to doing it again.

PICKING THE DATE

A reunion being planned for next year will have to take into considera-tion pre-scheduled events such as weddings, graduation parties, or vaca-tions. Any plans made before a future reunion date has been selected need to be discussed and accommodated. Unless the relative indicates their plans can be changed, eliminate that date. Keep a calendar handy to mark unacceptable times..

Yearly reunions are an effective way of keeping families connected. When picking a date seems too difficult at the time of the reunion, choose a time frame as a way to help everyone remember when the reunion will be held. You could designate the second Sunday in July as the day for all future reunions. Family functions are then less likely to be planned on that day and problems with conflicting schedules are unlikely to occur. Once a day is chosen, DO NOT change it or your relatives will be unable to count on a yearly scheduled reunion. If, one year, you change the reunion day to accommodate a baby shower, other family members will expect the same considerations for their future plans.

Scheduling the gatherings on exclusively odd or even numbered years, will help your relatives to keep track of when the reunions are being held. Condition your family members to think of the second Sunday of July in the *even* years as family reunion day. The easier you make it for people to remember when the next reunion is scheduled, the less likely they'll be to plan other activities for that day. When Uncle Bob accidentally sets up a golf tournament on reunion day, the other family members will be able to remind him ahead of time so *his* plans can be changed.

Scheduling the reunions for every five years may be the best option for families who are scattered throughout the country. This gives each family unit the opportunity to save the necessary money for traveling to and staying in the city where the reunion is being held.

THE NEXT REUNION SITE

After a decision is reached on when the next reunion is to take place, determine the location for the next party. Again, this should involve a group discussion with everyone present given the opportunity to express their preference.

Discuss how the location has influenced the number of people at the current reunion, and how any changes would improve attendance in the future. Be specific regarding problems with the current location so future sites can be analyzed. If the town is convenient, but there are problems with the site, now is the time to suggest keeping the geographic location but changing the area.

It's up to the current reunion planners to educate the guests on all that is involved in choosing a location. List everything that needs to be considered before choosing the location so people can make informed decisions. Remember, some of this was new to you just a few months ago! This is a list of considerations when selecting locations for future reunions:

- accommodations
- convenience
- cost
- recreation
- theme

If the relatives can't compromise on a location, put all the options in a hat and pick one. This works as well as any other method for making the decision and will prevent hurt feelings.

SUGGESTIONS FOR IMPROVEMENT

Ask those present their opinion on how to improve the next event. Encourage your relatives to write down their suggestions and put them into a box. Many people aren't comfortable raising their hand to give an opinion, so you'll probably get a better response if it's done anonymously.

There is no need to view any of these suggestions as negative feedback about the current reunion. This information is to be passed on to the next planners as reference material only.

Those who planned the current year's reunion may have had terrific ideas, but it'll be interesting and informative to see what the new group comes up with. Again, instead of being offended, just accept what is mentioned as suggestions for the future, not as complaints about the present.

Brainstorming is a good technique to come up with a variety of new and different ideas. The important thing to keep in mind is that no suggestion is a bad one. The main rule here is not to comment on any of the ideas until the end of the brainstorming session.

NEW PLANNING IDEAS

Now is the time to solicit different theme or setting ideas from your relatives. If the current reunion is in a park, a dinner dance or cruise may be suggested for the next meeting. Have someone write down the suggestions as they are being offered. Some of the ideas will seem difficult to plan, or won't be to your liking, but listen to all the ideas with an open mind. Remember, other family members may think the ideas are great and be willing to help in the planning.

Consider the cost to the participants when planning the next reunion. Give everyone a chance to put aside money before planning a costly reunion. Keep in mind a wide range of incomes is represented in your family. Make the reunion scheduling as convenient as possible so everyone can attend.

THE NEXT CHAIRPERSON

Having enjoyed planning the current reunion, you could offer to be chairperson the next time around. Volunteer your services immediately so relatives don't get nervous about being drafted into the position. The next reunion should be easier to plan, especially if it's a duplicate of the current reunion.

After all, the location has been researched and you know which activities were successful. The personalities of your relatives won't be a surprise the second time around, so you'll be able to anticipate the degree of their cooperation. Jump right in and offer your services, they'll certainly be appreciated!

On the other hand, you may be unable to help with the next reunion. Be very clear if you're available for consultation in any phase of the planning. Encourage your relatives to take on the challenge by describing the enjoyable aspects of planning the reunion. Stress the positive aspects of the job. When discussing problems, acknowledge they existed but explain how they were resolved.

TRANSFER THE INFORMATION

Plan to pass on the reunion reference material within two weeks. It isn't a good idea to turn over the records the day of the reunion since there's too much going on. Also, your job isn't done until after the reunion and you've filled in the final figures on the estimated cost/actual cost log.

Arrange a meeting with the new chairperson to explain all the material. Don't drop it off on their doorstep without any clues as to where you got your information and what they should do with it. Walk the new planner through the notebook and share helpful hints you picked up along the way.

Arrange to give this information to the next planner (especially if they are from another city) on a specified date. If mailed follow up a week after it was sent to confirm its arrival and review the contents. Make a copy of the material so you have it on hand when discussing it with the next planner.

ANNOUNCE ALL DECISIONS

Regardless of how the next planners are chosen, announce who they are before anyone leaves the reunion. When person has sole responsibility, make sure an alternate is named in case unforeseen circumstances force the original person to be unable to follow through. Suggest everyone write down the names and phone numbers of the planning committee as they are announced.

Before you leave, let everyone know the following information about the next get-together:

> Chairperson
> Date
> Location
> Time

This gives those who will attend something to look forward to and provides the future planners information to simplify their job. Make sure the final activity of the day is planning the basics of the next reunion. Keep the excitement level high throughout the day, but have your relatives absolutely buzzing with anticipation about the next reunion as they drive away!

LACK OF INTEREST

Be prepared for the slight possibility that your relatives may not show an interest in having another reunion. When a positive response response isn't forthcoming, it's best to drop the subject. It's not up to the current reunion planners to organize and plan all future family gatherings. Though disappointed, you can't take it personally if your relatives are unwilling to continue what you hoped would become a family tradition. As long as this reunion was planned to the best of your ability, hold your head high. The reason for the lack of interest probably has nothing to do with the current party, but instead involves work or family schedules, lack of money, or the unwillingness to devote the necessary time for the planning.

Store all of the paperwork and notebooks in a secure, waterproof box. In a few years, send postcards to those relatives who may be interested in having another reunion. Offer them the contents of the box and any support you're inclined to provide.

Family Newsletter

Family newsletters are becoming popular. If there is any interest in a newsletter for your family, now is the time to discuss the idea. Pre-addressed postcards can be distributed at the reunion. These should be returned by a specified date (which is noted on the card) and the newsletter will be compiled once a year from this information. Again, this takes time and money, so make sure you want to be involved in this sort of project before suggesting it to your family. You can also recruit family members who have desk-top publishing skills to help with the project.

Mini-Reunion

Sometimes when family reunions aren't scheduled on a yearly basis you may want to keep in contact with those relatives with whom you've found common interests. This can either be done with specific branches of the family or it can be arranged by generation. These gatherings will be smaller and less structured so they'll require less planning.

Set a date for this mini-reunion before leaving the family gathering. Once people leave the party, they are less inclined to follow through on planning the next meeting. Compare calendars and clearly mark the date for the next get-together.

Whether it's the mini-reunion or the annual reunion, write the information on December 20th on your current calendar (get together with Pedrey cousins June 12th) so it can be transferred to a new calendar. Send out notes or postcards a few weeks ahead of time to remind everyone of the gathering.

14

Update the Family Story

*W*henever we meet relatives, one thing always brought up is news of other family members. The same is true at family reunions. This event is a prime time to catch up on the news and to seek out a little more family history. As the reunion planner, you have the opportunity to encourage each family member to share their history and news with each other.

Questionnaires

An easy way to collect the news is to design a standard form. Each form should have a list of questions specific for each generation. Prepare questionaires for those just able to read and write through the oldest family member. When there are answers to the same questions to compare, relatives will be able to find similarities and differences within the branches and generations.

Ask Appropriate Questions

The questionnaire is your opportunity to learn as much as possible about your relatives in the least amount of time. Make the questions interesting to both the person filling out the form and those who will be reading it later. Make sure the questions asked are appropriate for the age group. It makes more sense to ask a senior citizen about their major life accomplishments rather than what they want to be when they grow up.

MAKE THE QUESTIONS FUN

After you get the basic information to identify each of your relatives, make the rest of the questions fun. Don't make people think too hard. This should remind anyone of taking a test in school. People are always more willing to participate in an activity that is fun. Anything that resembles work is usually set aside for another day.

QUESTIONNAIRE SAMPLES

The next few pages give questionnaire examples appropriate for a child, young adult, adult, and senior citizen. There is also an example everyone can fill out on reunion day. Use the samples to help develop biography sheets for your family.

TELL ME ABOUT YOURSELF
Ages 8 thru 13

Family Branch Name _____

Your Last Name _____First Name _____

Age _____ Nickname _____

1. My favorite thing to do when I'm not in school is _____

2. The most fun I have with my family is _____

3. If I could go anywhere in the world, I would go to _____
because _____

4. When I am 20 years old, I will _____

5. My favorite TV program is _____

6. I think school is _____

7. When I grow up I want to be _____ because _____

TELL ME ABOUT YOURSELF
Ages 14 thru 20

Family Branch Name _____

Your Last Name _____First Name _____

Age _____   Nickname _____

1. The funniest memory I have growing up in this family is _____

2. I wish my parents would let me _____

3. If I could plan our next vacation we would go to _____
because _____

4. Twenty years from now I will be living in _____
and I will be doing _____

5. My favorite form of entertainment is _____

6. I always thought it would be fun to _____
but once I tried it, I didn't like it because _____

TELL ME ABOUT YOURSELF
Ages 21 thru 64

Family Branch Name _____

Your Last Name _____First Name _____

Age _____   Nickname _____

Spouse's Name _____

Name(s) and Age(s) of Children _____

1. My proudest accomplishment, so far, has been _____

2. I spend my free time _____

3. My most exciting adventure was _____

4. If I had to do it again, the one thing I would do again is _____

5. Within the next 5 years, I am looking forward to _____

TELL ME ABOUT YOURSELF
over 65

Family Branch Name _____

Your Last Name _____ First Name _____

Age _____   Nickname _____

Spouses Name _____

Name(s) and Age(s) of Children _____

Name(s) and Age(s) of Grandchildren _____

Name(s) and Age(s) of Great-grandchildren _____

1. I enjoy spending time _____

2. My favorite memory of growing up in this family is _____

3. The one thing I still want to accomplish is _____

4. My proudest moment was _____

5. I regret _____

6. The silliest thing I ever did was when I was _____ years old and I ___

7. I want to be remembered as _____

TELL ME ABOUT YOURSELF
(Current year)

Family Branch Name _____

Your Last Name_____First Name _____

Age _____   Nickname _____

Spouse's Name _____

1. My hobbies are _____

2. The most interesting place I have ever been is _____
because _____

3. I like being a member of this family because _____

4. I can't wait until I _____

5. The most unusual thing I ever did was _____

6. This year I intend to _____

7. I am happiest when I _____

BEST TIME

Most people prefer a long time to complete a project once it's assigned to them. If the questionnaires are included with the invitations, relatives will be able to fill them out at their own pace. These should be returned prior to the reunion. Elderly relatives and younger children may need help in filling out their questionnaires. Because the forms are sent ahead of time, help can be given at a leisurely pace and free the reunion day for other activities. Having a few weeks to work on the project will insure more thoughtful responses.

WHO CAN'T ATTEND

Sending the questionnaire with the invitation allows relatives who are unable to attend the reunion an opportunity to still participate. Though not present, they'll be included in the information sharing portion of the day. Mail a biography sheet booklet to those who filled out the questionnaire but were unable to attend.

PRESENTING THE INFORMATION

Now that you've gathered everyone's life story, it's time to figure out how to pass this information along to the rest of the family. The advantage of receiving the responses prior to reunion day is that the question and answer sheets can be organized for distribution in advance of the event.

There are a variety of ways to organize the questionnaires when putting together your booklets. One way is to organize by family branch. The booklet is sectioned off with each branch being grouped together. The first sheet in each section would be the oldest family member of that branch. Following them would be their children, grandchildren, and great grandchildren. After each group has been featured, move on to the next family branch until all are covered.

A second option is to organize the questionnaires by age group. Since there are four different questionnaires based on age, it will be easy to tell who should be in each section.

When using this format, put the sheets in alphabetical order by first name. That way, upon meeting a new relative, you can quickly check the biography sheets and learn a little about them. Particularly memorable quotes and responses can be taken from the sheets and used elsewhere during the reunion.

EXTRA COPIES

Some family members won't have filled out their questionnaire but may want copies of the responses. Making a few extra copies to give out isn't going to provide a hardship to anyone. Besides, you want to promote good feelings and family harmony.

Keep the original copies of the questionnaires together in a hard covered binder labeled with the current year. Display this binder throughout the reunion. It's interesting to examine the books from past years to see how our views and opinions have changed as we've gotten older. Have the books available from previous reunions for anyone interested in taking a stroll down memory lane.

WHEN TO GIVE OUT THE BOOKLETS

One good time to distribute the booklets is when family members first arrive at the reunion. If you have a check-in point, keep the booklets there. The name of each person to receive a book should be written on the cover. Have the books organized alphabetically by last name so they are easy to find. The chief drawback to handing out the books upon arrival is that they must now be carried around during the reunion. Most people will, however, realize the information is worthy of the minor inconvenience.

These biography booklets can also be handed out as the relatives are leaving the reunion. Since the master copy is available during the event, it can be used as the reference source. This way the books won't be misplaced during the event. The major disadvantage is making sure everyone gets a booklet since relatives will be departing at various times.

THE QUESTIONNAIRE AS A REUNION ACTIVITY

It may be that the questionnaire can't be filled out ahead of time. Incorporate it into the activities on reunion day. This way you'll have a captive audience so it'll be harder for your relatives to refuse to participate.

Make sure the questions asked can be answered without a lot of thought because most of the family members will be distracted by the party activity. Choose a set of questions applicable to all groups so you only have one set of papers to be concerned about.

There are several options on how reunion day surveys can be distributed. First, you can have all the original questionnaires in the master-copy book. Since the book is available to everyone, those who are interested will take the time to examine it.

Secondly, you can gather all the completed questionnaires and deliver them to the copy shop. The problem here is missing the reunion to do paperwork. It may be difficult to get a volunteer, especially since no one will want to leave the party. There may not be a copy shop nearby—or it may be closed. If you choose this option, make sure you know the copy shop hours ahead of time. Shop around. Some shops feature pick up and delivery services. Arrange this service ahead of time.

Finally, though not cost effective, the survey can be mailed after the reunion. Along with the booklets, remind relatives of the name and phone number of the next chairperson as well as the next date and location.

Filling out the questionnaires and sharing the information is a good way of keeping up-to-date on your relative's. lives. By asking specific questions, you are helping to cement the blocks that build the history of your family.

MORE QUESTIONS THAT NEED ANSWERS

*A*fter reading this book, you still may have questions. I've tried to include as many of these miscellaneous questions as possible in this chapter so they can be addressed.

PETS

My great-aunt Marie won't go anywhere without her dog, Roc. How do I convince her to keep him home the day of the picnic?

Remind your aunt that pets are uncomfortable out of their familiar surroundings and probably would be happier at home. Mention that children, out of excitement, may play too rough with her dog so she'll have to keep it constantly with her. If she still insists after your conversation, consider Roc part of the family.

PROFESSIONAL PHOTOGRAPHER

Should we pay for a professional photographer?

You may want to have at least one group shot set up and photographed by a professional. This person has had experience with large groups and will be able to arrange everyone in an attractive pose. In years to come, it'll be fun to look back at the official photo album and have everyone in the photograph. If family members want to purchase photos, have them deal directly with the photographer.

INEXPENSIVE PHOTOGRAPHS

I can't afford the expense of a lot of professional photographs. How can I be in six places at once with my camera?

Buy a supply of disposable cameras and put them out at various reunion activity centers including game areas, on the dinner tables and near the guest of honor. Encourage your relatives to pick up the cameras and snap pictures any time. After the party, take all the cameras in to be developed at the same time. You'll have an instant family reunion album covering every aspect of the day.

FAMILY CHEFS

My family has lots of great cooks and I think it would be a neat idea to put together a professional looking family cookbook. How do I go about it? Will it be expensive?

Contact a local printer for help and direction. You can have everyone send in their recipes on paper the same size and only pay to have it bound. If enough copies are being printed, have it typeset or use a desk-publishing program to make your book. It'll probably cost less than you imagine so check it out. Make sure you give your cookbook a catchy title such as "Fava Family Favorites", prominently featuring the family name.

RELIGIOUS FAMILY MEMBERS

Some of my family members are quite religious. Is there anything special I can do for them?

Contact a priest, minister, or rabbi in the area where the reunion is to be held. Maybe a special service can be arranged, or your group could be singled out during the public service. Consider inviting the cleric to the meal to bless your food and lead the prayer. If the reunion is out of your area, and you're unsure who to call, look under churches in the Yellow Pages for help.

COMPUTER HELP

Will having a computer help me plan the reunion?

More and more people are purchasing home computers. These are terrific for mass producing personalized communications. Also, there are software programs able to perform a *merge* function to produce a mailing list. From this mailing list, you're able to make mailing labels. It's a great time saver to put on a label, rather than to hand-address envelopes. Many computer programs have banner making capabilities. This adds a personal touch to any event. Finally, if you have a computer, you're able to store all of your expense logs in the computer. This makes updating a snap. By all means, consider using a computer.

LOANING CAR TO RELATIVES

Quite a few of our relatives will be combining the reunion with their vacation. One family has asked if they can use our car. What do you recommend?

This is a tricky subject. First, before you offer your car to your brother-in-law Jack, check with your insurance agent to make sure any accident he becomes involved in is covered by your insurance policy. Second, insist he drive the car a few times while you are with him so you can show him any special features or idiosyncrasies of your vehicle. Third, remember—be nice, but be cautious when it comes to lending out your vehicle!

ENTERTAINING RELATIVES

How much should I volunteer to entertain out-of-town relatives after the reunion?

Hopefully you have a lot in common with your family members and will want to spend additional time with them. Plan activities you enjoy the week following the reunion and invite them to join you. This way, you'll be having a good time whether they're with you or not. If they suggest something you would rather not do, think of another family member who may be willing to participate with them. You may not want to walk through the woods, but your sister, Cathy, may enjoy being the trail guide.

TEENAGERS

What do we do with the teenagers?

Give them the opportunity to spend time together with minimal adult supervision. Allow them to play miniature golf, go bowling, spend the evening in a club, or just hang out at the mall. It's doubtful they're going to try anything troubling in the town where the reunion is being held that they haven't tried in their hometown. Trust them to behave and make sure they have the phone number where their parents can be reached.

A NECESSARY REUNION INGREDIENT

What is the most important ingredient in planning a successful family reunion?

The desire to be involved in the reunion will get you past the rough spots. As long as you keep an upbeat attitude and try your best, the reunion will be a success. Fortunately, there isn't a standard that you'll be measured against as to whether or not you're successful. Just being involved is a feather in your cap!

As you get involved with planning the reunion, more questions are bound to come up. Ask others who have had successful reunions how they handled similar situations. Then take your best guess and make a decision.

APPENDIX

A FAMILY TREE DIAGRAM

A family tree diagram like the example below will help identify who to invite to the reunion. The sample is set up with YOU being the one doing the tracking. From YOU, the generations and relatives can be recognized by their relationship to the planner. These include son, aunt, cousin, and grandmother.

FAUSTO FAMILY TREE

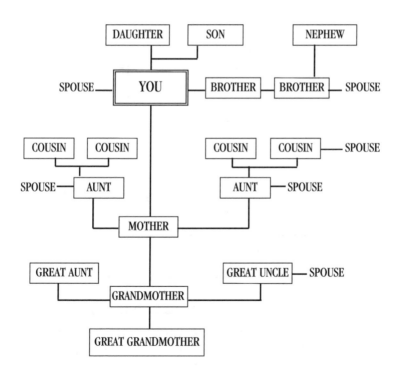

EXPENSE LOGS

The logs illustrate how to track your time and money. Only keep track of important information, otherwise you will get tired of writing down useless statistics. When creating the logs, keep them as basic as possible so you don't mind working on them.

Store all reunion material in the same binder. If everything is kept together there is no excuse not to use it on a daily basis. Remember, keep only reunion related material in this binder

ESTIMATED COST/ACTUAL COST LOG		
Item	Estimated Cost	Actual Cost
invitation printing	*$125.00*	*$132.25*

List item and estimated cost. Include postage, stationery, security deposit, room or park fee, and so forth.

PHONE LOG				
Date	Time	Name	Number Called	Length of Call
2/16	8:00 P.M.	Judy	(652)555-2734	7 Min.

Log all outgoing calls.

POSTAGE LOG		
DATE	REASON	COST
2/16	Roll of stamps	$29.00
	Total	_____

Log anything to do with mailing. Include stamps,
postcards, and mail weighed at post office.

MILEAGE LOG				
Date	Start	End	Total	Cost
2/16	8,712	8,916	204	$46.92
			Total	_____

Total Miles = ending milage–starting milage
Cost = Total Miles x .23 Per Mile

INVITATION EXAMPLES

The invitation is the first impression family members will get of the upcoming reunion. Regardless of how the invitation is presented, it will have an impact on your relatives. Now is when the creative, fun side of you can come out and be seen.

The examples include a handwritten invitation, a basic printed invitation to pass along information, and an invitation that a child can color. From these examples, you'll be able to design something that will appeal to your family.

Handwritten Invitation

Dear _____,

In case you didn't remember, it's reunion time! This is to let you know that I'm helping to plan our big event. The reunion date is set for _____ at _____ park. We plan to meet from _____A.M. until _____P.M.

Uncle Ken and Aunt Vara will be the guests of honor since they are celebrating their Golden Wedding Anniversary (50th) that month. Their sons, Paul and Mark, will be the masters of ceremony during the festivities.

We are asking for each family to bring a dish to pass—enough to feed eight people.

Please call me at (___)_____ and let me know whether or not your family plans to attend, the ages of the children attending, the food you plan to bring, and if you can help out the day of the reunion. If I'm not home, my answering machine can take a detailed message.

Activities will be held throughout the day, so plan to come and join in the fun.

With anticipation,

Arlene

Basic Printed Invitation

It's a Reunion
of the
Bodner Family

Date: _____

Time: _____

Locations: _____

Guest of Honor at this
year's festivities: _____

Please bring a current family photo
to display on the family tree.

Respond By: (_ _ _)_ _ _-_ _ _ _

Color By Hand Invitation

INVITATION LOG					
Name	SEND DATE	RSVP DATE	*1ST CALL	*2ND CALL	*3RD CALL
Lee Sherman	5/1	7/2	6/1	6/15	

Dates calls were placed to family member to confirm attendance.

INVITATION LOG – PART II				
NO. OF ADULTS	AGES 1–5	AGES 6–12	AGES 13+	*WILLING TO HELP
1				*Yes*

* Is the family member willing to help on Reunion Day?

INDEX

ABOUT THE AUTHOR

Nancy Funke Bagley, the second oldest of eight children, knows the pleasures of being surrounded by family. Her family and extended family have provided a lot of love, plenty of good times, and great memories of time spent together.

Nancy has a Bachelor of Science degree from Central Michigan University. She currently resides in North Carolina with her husband Richard and their two dogs, Molly and Yipee.